Lamb Country Cooking

Lamb with All the Trimmings

by Jill Stanford Warren

Original cover art by Elsa Warnick
Interior art by Cheryl Long
Cover design by PMH Design
Editorial Staff: Cheryl Long, Editor
            Maggie Ryan Vogt and Marlene King

LAMB COUNTRY COOKING: Lamb with All the Trimmings
Copyright © 1995 By Jill Stanford Warren.

Library of Congress Cataloging in Publications Data

Warren, Jill Stanford
Lamb Country Cooking: lamb with all the trimmings /
by Jill Stanford Warren.
        p. cm.
Includes index.
ISBN 0-914667-16-5
1. Cookery (Lamb and mutton) I. Title.
TX749.5.L35W37 1995
641.6'63--dc20   94-31657

Printed in   Published by:
The United States of America Culinary Arts Ltd.
                              P.O. Box 2157
                              Lake Oswego, Oregon 97035

Other Books by Culinary Arts Ltd. -
Gourmet Vinegars: How To Make & Cook With Them
Gourmet Mustards: How To Make & Cook With Them
Classic Liqueurs: The Art Of Making & Cooking With Liqueurs
The Best of Scanfest: A Treasury of Authentic Recipes & Proverbs
Easy Microwave Preserving

FIRST EDITION
95 96 97 98 99 - 10 9 8 7 6 5 4 3 2 1
Publisher's catalog available upon request

Table of Contents

About The Author

Jill Stanford Warren attended the Portland Art Museum School and Lewis & Clark College. A professional writer since 1976, she has been a contributing columnist for *The Mountain Newspaper* and *The Lariet*. She wrote and edited **Gray Power Magazine**. A feature writer for *The Senior Tribune*, she also wrote the Restaurant Review column. She became the Editor-in-Chief of the 10 edition, monthly paper.

Warren has been a feature writer for **Restaurateur Magazine** and **Pro Woman Magazine**, was formerly the Community Editor for the *Canby Herald* and Senior Editor for Hot Off The Press Publications. She is presently co-authoring a book, <u>Historic Restaurants of Oregon and Washington.</u>

Warren lives in the Oregon countryside in the Frederick Keil House, a National Historic Site. She is known as a gracious hostess and marvelous cook with great knowledge and flair in cooking lamb. A place at her oversized wide-planked dining table is a coveted place to be. The author credits her culinary appreciation of lamb and potatoes to her Irish heritage. The maternal side of her family came from Ireland to the United States in the 1700's.

Acknowledgments

No book writes itself, and this one is no exception. Thanks are given to: The American Lamb Council, The Oregon Lamb Council, Cheryl Long for encouraging me to write it, my husband, Roger, who ate *all* the recipes in this book, Lambs Thriftway in Wilsonville, Oregon, Howard Long for giving me 'the cold shoulder', Pearl Kosta at the Lake Oswego Public Library and last, to the wonderful people who shared their special recipes with me.

Jill Stanford Warren

Introduction

When I was growing up, Sunday dinner at my house was often a leg of lamb. We *always* had it at Easter. My mother cooked it the traditional way, with lots of garlic inserted into the meat and fresh rosemary from her herb garden sprinkled on top. She served it slightly pink. It was far and away my favorite dinner. My next favorite was lamb chops - crisp and flavorful. I can't remember a time I didn't like lamb.

But I have discovered that not everyone likes it. The world seems to be divided between the lovers and the haters - there is no middle ground. Perhaps this is because lamb is sometimes hard to find in the meat department, and there is the old stigma of tough old *mutton* hanging over it. But tender lamb and tough mutton are as different as night and day. And what do we do with lamb once we have it, anyway? This book should answer that question and many more.

There are numerous cuts of lamb and as many methods to cook them. This book is designed for the lamb lover who likes their lamb simple and good, as it ought to be. There are few recipes that call for ingredients you don't have right in your pantry. I have included some accompaniments that go well with a tender piece of lamb.

I hope the next time I am asked out to dinner, the host or hostess will serve a leg of lamb, slightly pink, with just a hint of garlic.

Jill Stanford Warren
Aurora, Oregon

"Of all birds, give me mutton*!"
Thomas Fuller

* the meat of fully grown sheep

All About Lamb

All About Lamb

No one knows who first domesticated the wild sheep that roamed the steppes and plains of Central Asia following the Ice Age. It is theorized that following a grass fire which caught many sheep in its path, early man ate the roasted meat and then sought to capture the sheep, eventually turning them into a herd. Archaeological digs have dated sheep bones as early as 9000 B.C.

Sheep were valuable for man, providing meat and an important source of protein and milk. The wool was woven into warm clothing to keep the nomadic peoples more comfortable, and it was waterproof as well. Sheep became an early status symbol–the more sheep you had, the wealthier you were.

Sheep can thrive in areas that would not support other animals, making them ideal for nomadic peoples always on the move. A man was judged by the size of his herd and sheep were obliging by having two and sometimes three lambs per year.

Man kept on the move by following the herds as they roamed for grass. New lands opened up as the first shepherds went in search of new pastures.

Unlike beef and pork, there are few religious prejudices about lamb. In fact, for some religions, lamb is a symbol of purity. Lamb has been associated with two of the world's great religions, Christianity and Judaism. Christ is symbolized as the lamb in Christian tradition. The Jews place a lamb shank on the Passover platter commemorating the pascal lamb sacrificed when the Angel of Death was said to have flown over Egypt, slaying the first born sons of Egyptians, but sparing the Hebrews.

The Chinese believe lamb gives the body heat. Lamb is still the most popular meat in the Middle East, Northern Africa and Greece. The Italians have a milk-fed lamb they are passionate about, and the French - those magicians of the culinary arts - are simply wild over lamb which they call *gigot*. In France, 48% of the people prefer lamb over all other types of meat!

In 1913, French restaurateur, Charles Sébillon, opened his restaurant, the Belle 'Epoque, and put lamb on the menu. Today, the restaurant serves 35 legs of lamb each day, 8,600 legs a year from the Limousin region of France.

American chefs have not been left behind. Nearly half of all upscale restaurants offer lamb on their menus. Lamb appears in meat markets in a wide variety of cuts.

Lamb can be an elegant company dish or a hearty family-style dinner. Whatever your choice, lamb deserves a place on the menu each week.

This book is designed to help you discover (or re-discover!) lamb. I have concentrated on cuts which are easily obtained from the butcher. As so often happens, there are leftovers to deal with, and here are some delectable solutions. What goes with lamb? Many wonderful foods; refer to the accompaniment chapter for inspiration.

To quote Julia Child who said it better than anyone else, "Bon Appetit!"

All About Lamb

Glossary of Lamb Terms:
• **Chops** - meat with bone that has been sliced from the leg, usually 1-inch thick.
• **Fell** - the paper-like covering over the fat. This is generally removed prior to cooking smaller pieces of lamb, like a chop, but is left on to retain juiciness on roasts and legs, then removed before carving.
• **Loin** - the tender strip of lean meat cut from the rib.
• **Medallion** - a round or oval slice.
• **Saddle** - a roast that consists of a pair of whole loins.
• **Shank** - the lower end of the leg.
• **Spring Lamb** - lamb that is under 1 year old. Good quality lamb has firm flesh. The fat is very white and the ends of the bones are red, appear porous and moist. More mature lamb has whiter, drier bones and darker meat.

Buying Lamb:
• The most tender cuts, with the mildest flavor, come from the back, rib and loin where the muscles are not worked. Shoulders and shanks will be less tender and have a stronger flavor.
• The American Lamb Council recommends portions ranging from 3-4 to 6-8 ounces of boneless lamb per person, and 4-6 to 8-12 ounces with bone, depending on appetites and the desired amount of protein required. Adjust the portions according to your healthy choices.
• Lamb may be stored, tightly wrapped, in the refrigerator two to four days or in the freezer for six to nine months for optimum flavor. Fresh ground lamb should be used within two days, or may be frozen for up to four months.

Preparing Lamb:
• Trim fat before cooking, as lamb fat has a strong flavor.
• Lamb tenderizes by marinating in lemon juice, orange juice or flavored vinegars.

Buying a whole or half lamb from a retail/wholesale meat processor can be economical, and it allows you to obtain exactly the cuts you want. Look in the yellow pages of your telephone book under 'meat'. Call and ask when they will have lamb available. Usually, lamb can be purchased all through the spring, summer and into early fall.

Spring lambs used to be ready at 4 to 5 months for Easter. Today's lambs are usually 5 to 6 months old and are born later in the spring. They will weigh 90 to 140 pounds, live weight, depending on the breed of sheep and the genetics of their parents.

You can purchase either a half or whole lamb. If you have the freezer space, I recommend buying lamb directly. Why not go in with a friend and split the costs and the meat?

Nearly half the weight of the lamb is lost from live to hanging. The price you will pay is based on the hanging weight of the lamb. After the lamb is cut to your specifications, there will be a 10% to 15% drop in weight. This is from the removal of bones, excess fat and other waste.

As an example, I purchased a whole lamb that weighed in at 58 pounds, hanging weight. After cutting and wrapping, my lamb weighed approximately 31 pounds. The price of the live lamb, the cutting, extra boning and wrapping has made a savings of approximately 40% for the amount of lamb that I specifically wanted-2 legs, cut in half, 2 boned and rolled shoulders, 8 packages of rib chops and 2 packages of shoulder chops (4 to a package) and 6 pounds of ground lamb.

The butcher will do exactly what you want, in the number and cuts you specify. Study the charts on the next page to determine how you would like your lamb dressed out. And don't be afraid to ask questions!

Basic Cuts

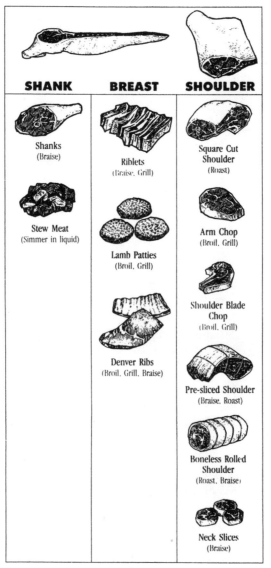

SHANK	BREAST	SHOULDER
Shanks (Braise)	Riblets (Braise, Grill)	Square Cut Shoulder (Roast)
Stew Meat (Simmer in liquid)	Lamb Patties (Broil, Grill)	Arm Chop (Broil, Grill)
	Denver Ribs (Broil, Grill, Braise)	Shoulder Blade Chop (Broil, Grill)
		Pre-sliced Shoulder (Braise, Roast)
		Boneless Rolled Shoulder (Roast, Braise)
		Neck Slices (Braise)

Courtesy of the American Lamb Council

RACK

Rack Roast
(Roast)

Rib Chops
(Broil, Grill)

French Rib Chops
(Broil, Grill)

Rack for One
(Roast)

Double French Rack
(Roast)

LOIN

Loin Chop
(Broil, Grill)

Loin Roast
(Roast)

Double Loin Chop
(Broil, Grill)

Medallion
(Broil)

Boneless Loin
(Roast)

SIRLOIN

Sirloin Roast
(Roast)

Sirloin Steaks
(Broil, Grill)

Sirloin Shank Half
(Roast)

Cubes for Shish
Kabob
(Broil, Grill)

Boneless Sirloin
(Roast, Broil, Grill)

LEG

Whole Leg
(Roast)

Round Leg Steak
(Braise, Broil, Grill)

Boneless Leg
(Oven Roast, Spit
Roast)

3/4 French Style
Leg
(Roast)

Shank Half
(Roast)

Butterflied Leg
(Broil, Grill)

Roasting & Broiling

Lamb Cut	Oven Temperature	Cooking time Minutes Per Pound
*Leg, bone in	325°F	17 to 20-rare 21 to 24-medium-rare 24 to 30-medium to well
*Leg, boneless rolled and tied	325°F	25 to 30-rare 30 to 35-medium-rare 35 to 37-medium
*Shoulder, boneless rolled and tied	325°F	30 to 35-rare 35 to 38-medium-rare 38 to 40-medium
*Rib roast, rack	325°F	25 to 30-rare 30 to 35-medium-rare 35 to 37-medium
*Crown roast, stuffed	325°F	18 to 20-rare 20 to 24-medium-rare 25 to 30-medium

Cuts	Minutes Per Side
Loin chops, 3/4-inch thick	3-rare 4-medium 5-well done
Loin chops, 1 1/2-inch thick	4-rare 5-medium 6- well done
Shoulder chops, 1-inch thick	4-rare 5-medium 6-well done

*Internal temperatures - For rare 140°F,
for medium-rare 150°F, for medium to well 160°F.

Herbs & Spices* that enhance lamb dishes are:

allspice	*fennel*	*sage*
basil	*fenugreek*	*saffron threads*
bay leaves	*fine herbes*	*salt*
bouquet garni	*garlic*	*shallots*
cardamom	*ginger*	*tarragon*
chili peppers	*lemon peel*	*thyme*
chives	*marjoram*	*watercress*
chervil	*mint*	*5-spice powder*
cilantro	*mustards*	
cinnamon	*nutmeg*	
cloves	*oregano*	
coriander	*paprika*	
cumin	*parsley*	
curry powder	*peppers*	
dill weed	*rosemary*	

*Check dried herbs stored for more than a year. They tend to lose their flavor and may need to be replaced.

Nutritional Benefits:

Health-conscious cooks know that trimmed lamb is low in calories and a highly nutritious source of protein. One trimmed, cooked 3-ounce serving contains 176 calories. This same 3-ounce serving provides about one-third of the total daily protein recommended for an adult. Lamb is a valuable source of iron, in the form of easily absorbable heme iron, as well as niacin, vitamin B-12 and zinc.

Lean, cooked lamb contains approximately 9% intra-muscular fat which enhances its flavor.

Easter Dinner

Tomato Aspic with Shrimp & Dilled Mayonnaise
America's Favorite Leg of Lamb, page 18
English Mint Sauce, page 113
Roasted Potatoes with Garlic & Rosemary, page 120
Steamed Asparagus
Easter Egg Angel Food Cake

Simple Supper

Lamb Chops - Garlic Chops, page 42 **or**
Buffet Chops, page 34 **or** Swiss Chops, page 41
Apple-Mint Chutney, page 112
Daffodil Rice, page 118
Sautéed Zucchini Slices
Beefsteak Tomato Slices with Basil

A Summer Barbecue

Hans' Sure-Fire Barbecued Loin of Lamb, page 60
Corn on the Cob
Casserole of Eggplant & Lamb, page 70
Ice Cream Sundaes

Monday Night Dinner

Basque Sandwiches -
Cold Roast Lamb in Pita Bread with
Homemade Mayonnaise and Salt & Pepper to taste
Tuscany Bean Soup, page 121

Winter Dinner

Moroccan Lamb Stew, page 79
Cranberry Chutney, page 110
Crusty French Bread

Cooking
Prime Cuts

America's Favorite Leg of Lamb

*If you ask anyone how they like their Sunday lamb, the answer
will probably be this tried and true way of preparing it. Lamb
roast, roasted potatoes and herbed lamb gravy are all in this
perfect oven meal. Serve with petite peas. 8 to 10 servings.*

1 (5-pound) leg of lamb, trimmed of excess fat
3 cloves of garlic, peeled and slivered
1 tablespoon olive oil
1 tablespoon fresh snipped rosemary **or** 1 teaspoon dried
  rosemary, crumbled
1 1/2 teaspoons salt **or** to taste
1 1/2 teaspoons pepper
4 potatoes, washed, peeled and cut into quarters
1/2 cup beef broth, reserved

Preheat oven to 325°F. With the tip of a sharp knife, cut
small slits all over the leg of lamb. Insert garlic slivers into
the slits. Brush leg with olive oil. Sprinkle with rosemary,
salt and pepper.

Put lamb in a shallow roasting pan placing potatoes around
it. Roast at 325° for 1 1/2 to 2 hours, or until internal temperature is 160 to 180 degrees F. Turn potatoes occasionally so
they will brown evenly.

Remove roast and potatoes from pan to a serving platter.
Cover with foil to keep warm.

Add beef broth to remaining juices in the roasting pan,
stirring and scraping up the bits of roasted meat. Bring to a
boil, and reduce heat to a simmer. Stir often until liquid is
slightly thickened.

Apricot–Glazed Lamb

Apricots lend a sunny note to the glaze on this fruited leg of lamb. 6 servings.

1 (4-pound) leg of lamb, trimmed of excess fat
1 teaspoon salt
$1/2$ teaspoon pepper
2 teaspoons powdered ginger
$1/2$ teaspoon nutmeg
1 cup apricot preserves
2 tablespoons mint jelly

Preheat oven to 325°F. Place the leg of lamb in a shallow roasting pan. With a sharp knife, score fat in diagonal slices. Sprinkle spices over the roast. Combine the remaining ingredients, and pour over half the lamb. Roast for 1 hour and 20 minutes for medium-well doneness. Baste lamb frequently with the remaining apricot-mint sauce.

Variations:
Use apple jelly, peach preserves, red currant jelly, apricot-ginger chutney or pear marmalade, instead of the apricot preserves.

Herbed Leg of Lamb

Pull out all the stops for your next dinner party with this herb-encrusted roast surrounded by colorful spring vegetables. Use your imagination with the vegetables - if asparagus is not available, use green peppers. Try turnips and carrots for good color and flavor. Serve this with a Merlot wine for guaranteed thank-you notes! 8 to 10 servings.

1 (8-pound) leg of lamb, trimmed of excess fat
2 tablespoons olive oil

Herb Crust:
1 teaspoon dried thyme
1 teaspoon dried basil
1 teaspoon dried rosemary
1 teaspoon dried tarragon
1 teaspoon dried marjoram
1 teaspoon dried oregano
4 teaspoons dried parsley
$^1/_2$ teaspoon fresh ground black pepper

Vegetables:
16 small red potatoes, par-boiled
16 garlic cloves, peeled
16 small white onions, peeled and par-boiled
16 stalks of spring asparagus, par-boiled
16 pieces of yellow pepper, cut in 1-inch pieces

Lamb Gravy:
2 tablespoons lamb drippings from pan
$^1/_2$ cup dry red wine
1 cup beef broth
$^1/_2$ cup half-and-half*

* Lower calorie/fat option - substitute canned evaporated skimmed milk for the half-and-half.

Preheat oven to 450°F. Insert a meat thermometer into the thickest part of the roast; be careful not to touch the bone. Score fat with a sharp knife in diagonal cuts (as for a ham, for instance). Brush roast with olive oil and sprinkle herbs over, pressing them onto the oil to form a crust. Place the roast in a shallow pan and roast at 450°F for 10 minutes.

Reduce heat to 350°F and roast for 90 minutes. Remove leg of lamb from oven and place the vegetables around roast. Continue to cook for 1 hour, turning the vegetables occasionally so they will brown evenly. When the meat thermometer registers 160°F (medium-well done), remove roast to a serving platter placing cooked vegetables around it. Hold in a warm place while preparing the gravy.

Gravy:
Drain off fat from the pan except 2 tablespoons. Add wine and stir, scraping up all the roasted bits. Cook until it is reduced by half. Add beef broth and cook until it is again reduced by half, stirring often. Add half-and-half and cook until the gravy coats the back of a spoon. Adjust seasonings, if necessary.

Irish Lamb with Rosemary

*My friend, Michael of Dublin, was invited to a dinner at
Springfort Hall, near Mallow, in County Cork, Ireland. His
host, Michael Cooper, served this delicious leg of lamb with
rosemary so everyone would remember the special evening.
The Springfort Hall farm lamb has the unusual variation of
being basted with sherry. The strained juices may be served as
gravy. 8 servings.*

1 (5-pound) leg of lamb, trimmed of excess fat
3 garlic cloves, cut into slivers
1/4 cup olive oil
1/4 teaspoon salt
1/2 teaspoon pepper
4 sprigs fresh rosemary **or** 2 tablespoons dried
1 cup sweet sherry

Preheat oven to 325°F. Insert slivers of garlic into small
gashes made over the leg of lamb with the point of a very
sharp knife. Brush lamb with olive oil and sprinkle salt and
pepper over the top. Tie fresh sprigs of rosemary to the leg,
or if using dried rosemary, sprinkle all over leg.

Place lamb into preheated oven for 15 to 20 minutes per
pound. Baste halfway through cooking with sweet sherry.

Wide Awake Lamb

I don't suppose it makes any difference if you use regular or decaffeinated coffee in this recipe. At least, decaf worked for me. 6 servings.

1 (5-pound) leg of lamb, well-trimmed of fat
2 garlic cloves, peeled
1 teaspoon dried oregano **or** rosemary
$^1/_2$ teaspoon salt
$^1/_2$ teaspoon pepper
1 cup strong black coffee

Preheat oven to 350°F. Rub lamb with garlic cloves, then sprinkle on the herbs and spices. Roast lamb in a shallow roasting pan, allowing 20 minutes per pound. Baste with coffee at 15 minute intervals.

Variation:
In England (I swear this is true!), they use coffee with milk and sugar in it to produce a sugary-sweet, almost caramelized glaze. It's quite good for those with a sweet tooth.

Basil-Nut Pesto
Stuffed Leg of Lamb

Fresh basil lends its own special character to this pesto. (A prepared pesto works well, if you're in a hurry.) Nice served with fresh pasta and a spinach salad. 6 to 8 servings.

1 (5-pound) leg of lamb, boned and rolled

Pesto:
1 cup fresh basil, torn into pieces
4 tablespoons walnuts
2 cloves garlic
¼ cup olive oil
1 tablespoon olive oil
1 teaspoon salt
1 teaspoon pepper

Preheat oven to 350°F. Place basil, walnuts, garlic and ¼ cup olive oil in a food processor or blender. Blend at high speed for 1 minute. Carefully unroll roast and spread pesto onto the center. Re-roll and re-net the roast.

Brush roast with the tablespoon of olive oil and season with salt and pepper to taste. Roast at 350°F for 12 to15 minutes per pound. Let stand at room temperature for 15 minutes before slicing.

Herb & Garlic Stuffed Leg of Lamb

This festive entrée is good served with a special rice pilaf. Ask your butcher to prepare a boned and rolled leg of lamb. Serves 10 to 12.

1 (6-pound) boneless leg of lamb
$1/2$ cup fresh chopped parsley
2 tablespoons fresh chopped green onions
1 tablespoon chopped fresh thyme **or** 1 teaspoon dried
$1/4$ teaspoon salt
$1/4$ teaspoon pepper
$1/2$ cup fresh white bread crumbs
2 cloves garlic, peeled and minced

Preheat oven to 325°F. Mix herbs, spices and garlic together with bread crumbs and spread evenly over the inside of the roast. Carefully re-roll and re-net roast. Place roast on a rack in a roasting pan and bake for 20 minutes per pound.

To serve, cut netting away from the meat and discard it. Slice meat so the interior of the herbed bread crumbs are in the center of each serving slice.

Lamb Rack with Hazelnuts

Hazelnuts used to be called filberts. These nuts, by any name, are wonderful to use in cooking. The Oregon Hazelnut Marketing Board kindly shared this tempting and slightly nutty-flavored recipe. 4 servings.

1 (3-pound) rack of lamb, trimmed of excess fat
$1/4$ cup vegetable oil
2 tablespoons ground hazelnuts
$1/2$ teaspoon salt
$1/2$ teaspoon pepper
$1/3$ cup chopped roasted hazelnuts*
3 dried figs, coarsely chopped

Preheat oven to 400°F. Rub the rack with 2 tablespoons of oil. With fork tines, press ground hazelnuts onto meat. Season with salt and pepper. Heat oil in a large sauté pan until hot. Place rack, meat side down in the pan and brown well. Turn over and place the pan in the oven for 15 to 20 minutes. Remove the rack and allow to sit for 5 minutes.

Arrange the rack in a circular fashion. Garnish the center with chopped, roasted hazelnuts and dried figs.

*To roast hazelnuts, chop them coarsely and put on a baking sheet in a 350°F oven for 10 minutes.

Marinated Rack of Lamb

An unusual combination of ingredients combine to make a marinade you will dream about. Summer or winter, a salad of fresh greens with a simple oil and vinegar dressing is a nice, cool accompaniment to this flavorful meat with a loaf of French bread. 8 servings.

1 (8-pound) rack of lamb, trimmed of excess fat

Burgundy Marinade: *(Yields 2^1/$_2$-quarts to reuse on other meats, fish or poultry. If not using immediately, freeze.)*
1^1/$_2$ cups soy sauce
^{1}/$_4$ cup Worchestershire sauce
2 cups Burgundy wine
1 cup chopped onion
1 teaspoon garlic salt
1^1/$_2$ teaspoons pepper
1^1/$_2$ teaspoons oregano
^{1}/$_3$ cup fresh lemon juice

Combine all ingredients. Marinate rack of lamb approximately 6 hours, turn at least once.

Preheat oven to 350°F. Place rack, fat side up, on a broiling pan and bake for 50 minutes.

Remove rack and cut off the top layer of fat. Place rack on a hot barbecue grill or in your oven for 15 minutes, basting with additional marinade.

Saucy Hazelnut Lamb Rack

Oregon hazelnuts are a key ingredient in this unusual rack of lamb that features a hazelnut sauce. Fresh fettucine is my choice to accompany this excellent dish. 4 servings.

1 (3-pound) rack of lamb, trimmed of excess fat
2 cups unsalted chicken stock
$1/2$ cup dry white wine
$1/2$ teaspoon salt
$1/2$ teaspoon pepper
2 small turnips, peeled and diced
1 tablespoon vegetable oil
$1/3$ cup chopped roasted hazelnuts*

Preheat oven to 450°F. To make sauce, combine chicken stock and wine in a small saucepan and boil rapidly until reduced by half, about 10 minutes. Add salt, pepper and turnips. Simmer until turnips are tender. Set aside.

Brush the bottom of a heavy skillet or roasting pan with oil. Set pan over high heat and quickly sear the lamb on all sides. Place meat in an ovenproof pan and roast for 10 to15 minutes. This produces a medium-well done lamb rack.

Stir roasted hazelnuts into the sauce and reheat. Slice rack into six servings, and spoon sauce over the meat.

*To roast hazelnuts, chop them coarsely and put on a baking sheet in a 350°F oven for 10 minutes.

Minted Marinated Crown

Mint seems to be a perfect herb for lamb - its cool flavor marries with the richness of the meat. 4 servings.

1 (8-pound) crown, (2 or 3 ribs per serving)
1/4 teaspoon salt
1/4 teaspoon pepper

Mint Marinade:
1/2 cup mint sauce*
1 cup white rice wine vinegar
2 tablespoons olive oil
1/3 cup lemon juice
4 cloves garlic, crushed
1 cup sliced white onion
2 bay leaves
2 tablespoons dried and crumbled mint leaves
1 teaspoon dried thyme
Fresh mint sprigs for garnish (optional)

Combine all ingredients for the marinade in a bowl large enough to hold the crown roast. Marinate for at least 12 hours (overnight works best). Turn roast occasionally.

Preheat oven to 350°F. Remove roast from marinade and sprinkle with salt and pepper. Roast for 2 hours, basting with marinade every 30 minutes.

*See page 113 to make your own.

Easter Crown of Lamb

This is a favorite at our house at Easter. We always serve small red potatoes in parsley butter and fresh asparagus with it. 6 servings.

1 (6-pound) crown roast, well-trimmed
$1/4$ teaspoon salt
$1/4$ teaspoon pepper

Herb Stuffing:
$1/2$ cup chopped celery
$1/2$ cup chopped onion
2 tablespoons butter **or** margarine
1 beef bouillon cube
$1^1/2$ cups hot water
4 cups unseasoned dry bread cubes **or** stuffing cubes
1 carrot, coarsely grated
1 teaspoon salt
$1/4$ teaspoon pepper
$1/4$ teaspoon marjoram
1 egg, beaten

Preheat oven to 325°F. Season crown with salt and pepper. Place roast, ribs ends down, on a rack and bake for $1^1/2$ hours.

To make the stuffing:
Sauté celery and onion in butter. Dissolve bouillon cube in hot water and combine it with all the remaining ingredients, mixing well. Remove the roast from oven and turn so that rib ends are up. Turn rack into a circle and fill the inside with stuffing. Return to oven for an additional 1 to $1^1/2$ hours, or until desired doneness is reached.

Wine Choices

Thinking about wine in combination with Jill Stanford Warren's marvelous lamb recipes is a delight. Lamb's flavor, aroma and texture goes beautifully with a variety of wines. Many of these recipes are for special occasions, and the occasions will seem more festive if you serve wine, too.

Most lamb dishes demand red wines, because red wines are hearty enough to stand up to lamb's strong, distinctive flavors. Here is a brief description of several popular red wines, and the sorts of lamb dishes that they will complement. (If you're not a red wine drinker, skip to the end for a few alternatives.)

Cabernet Sauvignon, with its deep, ruby color and flavors of berries, mint and black pepper, works well with grilled or roast lamb. When young, these wines can be somewhat tannic and bitter; ask your wine merchant to recommend one that's 'accessible' or 'drinking well'. The French equivalent is Bordeaux -- it's a classic with sauces that include Roquefort cheese, which comes from the same region of France. I'd also try it with recipes that emphasize mint.

Merlot is quickly gaining on Cabernet Sauvignon in popularity, because it is often more drinkable young, with lovely berry and cherry flavors. The Merlot grape is also used in Bordeaux wines. Try Washington State or California Merlots with herb-baked lamb chops or leg of lamb.

Pinot Noir, the grape used in Burgundy (Bourgogne on French labels), makes a delicious red wine that would go with practically any lamb dish. It may be the most versatile of all red wines. Some Pinot Noirs can be pricey, so ask your wine merchant for help choosing one that's fruity, not too acidic and a good value. Heavenly with garlic anything.

Wines

Syrah comes mostly from the northern Rhone Valley of France. Look for labels like St. Joseph and Cornas, or Cotes-du-Rhone (great value wines that are often blended with other grapes). Syrah is known for a peppery quality and a deep ruby color; try it with Jill's lamb chops with lemon pepper and oregano. In Australia, the grape is called Shiraz, and the wines are yummy.

Zinfandel is grown only in the United States. It makes a robust wine that works well with stews, grills and strong flavors. The best Zinfandels have the aromas of berry, black pepper, raisin and even soy -- try it with Teriyaki.

If you don't drink red wine, choosing wine for lamb is a little more difficult, but not impossible. Look for oak-aged Chardonnays, which have lovely buttery and vanilla aromas along with the classic fruit and spice flavors. With sweet lamb dishes, try Alsatian Gewurztraminer or very slightly sweet wines like German Riesling. For a real change, seek out some dry Sherry -- yes, I mean dry, like fino or amontillado -- which has body and complex flavors which stand up to hearty lamb.

As you may have guessed, I'm a big believer in finding a good wine merchant and taking his or her advice. Never be afraid to say what you're cooking and how much you want to spend; a good wine merchant will be happy to help you. (If you find one of the rare wine snobs, go elsewhere.) You may pay a dollar more than supermarket prices at a specialty wine shop, but knowledgeable assistance is worth its weight in, well, lamb chops. Cheers!   Heidi Yorkshire

Heidi Yorkshire is the author of **Wine Savvy: The Simple Guide to Buying and Enjoying Wine Anytime, Anywhere.** She contributes to *Bon Appetit,* the *Wine Spectator* and *Travel & Leisure.*

Chops,
Steaks & Shanks

Buffet Chops

This was always a staple item on my mother's buffet menu. You can increase the number of chops to match the size of your buffet. 4 servings.

4 (4-ounce) lamb chops, boned
4 strips lean bacon
4 toothpicks
1/4 cup Worcestershire sauce

Preheat oven to 350°F. Wrap a strip of bacon around each chop and fasten with a toothpick. Brush tops of chops with Worcestershire sauce and bake them on a rack for 35 minutes, or until bacon is crisp.

Danish Blue Lamb Chops

Blue cheese adds a zip to the chops. 4 servings.

8 loin **or** rib lamb chops, 1 to 2-inches-thick
2 tablespoons olive oil
1 teaspoon salt
1 teaspoon pepper
1 clove of garlic, minced
1/2 cup Danish blue cheese **or** other strong blue cheese
2 tablespoons thick cream

Preheat the broiler. Brush chops on both sides with oil. Sprinkle with salt and pepper and spread minced garlic onto both sides of chops.

Mix cream and cheese together to form a paste. Broil the chops for 5 to 6 minutes on each side. Remove from broiler and spread the cheese mixture on one side of each chop. Replace under broiler until cheese is light brown and bubbling.

Honey-Mustard Lamb Chops

*If you want to make your own Dijon mustard for this recipe,
check out a great book by Helene Sawyer called,* **Gourmet
Mustards** *(Culinary Arts Ltd., Publishers). 2 servings.*

4 (4-ounce) loin chops, well-trimmed of fat
1 clove garlic
2 teaspoons fresh **or** $1/2$ teaspoon dried rosemary
$1/4$ teaspoon pepper
2 tablespoons honey
1 tablespoon Dijon-style mustard

Cut garlic clove in half and rub chops with the cut side. Press
rosemary and pepper onto both sides of chops. Place chops
on a broiler rack. Stir honey and mustard together, set aside.
Broil chops for 4 minutes; turn them over and spread with
honey-mustard. Broil 4 minutes more, longer if you prefer
well done meat.

Plum Perfect Chops

*I created this recipe last summer, when I had more preserves
than jars and decided to improvise. 4 servings.*

4 (4-ounce) loin chops, well-trimmed of fat
2 teaspoons lemon juice
$1/2$ teaspoon salt
$1/2$ teaspoon pepper
$1/2$ cup plum preserves

Rub lemon juice onto chops and arrange them in a shallow
oiled baking dish. Broil for 4 minutes and turn them over.
Sprinkle them with salt and pepper. Broil for 2 minutes.
Spread plum preserves over and broil for an additional 2
minutes, or until done.

Laura's Basque Lamb Chops

My friend, Laura, draws upon her Basque shepherding heritage for this surprising recipe that marries the flavors of Spain and France. She says Roquefort makes the difference! 2 servings.

4 (1-inch-thick) loin chops, well-trimmed of fat
4 tablespoons butter, melted
4 tablespoons Roquefort cheese
4 tablespoons flour
1 teaspoon salt
1 teaspoon pepper
2 tablespoons Worcestershire sauce
2 tablespoons water

Rub the chops with melted butter, and sprinkle cheese on them. Pat the flour onto the top of the chops with the back of a spoon. Sprinkle the chops with the salt and pepper.

Broil in a preheated broiler for 5 minutes. Remove from heat. Turn chops over and broil for another 5 minutes. Pour over the chops a sauce made with the Worcestershire sauce and water. Broil the chops 5 minutes longer.

Omar Kayam Lamb

*A taste of the Middle East makes this an exotic dish to serve.
Try it with the Mint Riata on page 114. 4 servings.*

4 (3- to 4-ounces) rib chops, trimmed of excess fat
4 tablespoons olive oil, divided
1 cup cracked (bulgur) wheat
1 cup chicken broth
1 onion, diced
1 cup carrot, diced
1 cup celery, diced
1 teaspoon salt
1 teaspoon pepper
2 teaspoons curry powder*
4 tablespoons cornstarch
1 cup water

Brown cracked wheat in 2 tablespoons of olive oil in a large
skillet. Transfer to a baking dish. Heat remaining olive oil
and brown onion and chops, turning them frequently. Season
with salt, pepper and curry powder. Add cornstarch and
water, stirring until thickened. Adjust seasonings, if necessary.

Preheat oven to 350°F. Place browned chops and onion on
top of wheat in baking dish. Add carrots and celery. Pour
gravy over all and bake 1 hour in preheated oven.

*See page 117 to make your own curry powder.

Pepper Chops

The colors of the peppers make this an attractive dish to serve, as well as being very flavorful. 2 servings.

4 (1½-inch-thick) loin chops, trimmed of excess fat
2 tablespoons olive oil, divided
½ cup white onion, sliced
1 clove garlic, peeled and minced
1 cup red bell pepper, cut into strips
1 cup green bell pepper, cut into strips
1 cup yellow bell pepper, cut into strips
1 cup diced tomato
2 tablespoons dried basil
1 teaspoon salt
1 teaspoon pepper
1 cup beef broth
2 tablespoons balsamic vinegar

Heat 1 tablespoon oil in a skillet. Add chops and sauté over medium-high heat until browned. Remove to a platter and pour off any excess fat.

Heat remaining oil in skillet and sauté onion and garlic. Add peppers and sauté for 2 minutes. Stir in tomato, basil, salt, pepper, broth and vinegar. Turn up heat, bring to a boil and add chops. Simmer chops in vegetable broth for 2 to 4 minutes.

Remembrance Lamb

Wine, rosemary and apples get it together for this fragrant lamb dish. Wide egg pasta provides the perfect counterpoint. 6 servings.

2¹/₂ pounds boneless loin of lamb, cut into 6 slices
¹/₄ cup vegetable oil
¹/₄ teaspoon salt
¹/₄ teaspoon pepper
Wide egg noodles (optional)

For the Sauce:
2 cups Cabernet Sauvignon wine
1 cup chicken stock
2 scallions, chopped
2 cloves garlic, peeled and chopped
2 cups heavy cream
3 tart apples, peeled, cored and chopped
1 tablespoon Dijon-style mustard
1 tablespoon fresh rosemary **or** ¹/₂ teaspoon, dried

Preheat oven to 375°F. Heat oil in skillet and sear lamb on both sides. Transfer lamb to an ovenproof platter and roast in oven for 10 minutes. Remove from oven and transfer to a serving platter. Cover the lamb and allow to 'rest' while the sauce is being made.

Simmer wine, chicken stock, scallions and garlic until they are reduced by half (about 30 minutes). Add cream, apples, mustard and rosemary. Allow to simmer for an additional 15 to 20 minutes, or until slightly thickened. For each serving, make a nest of cooked noodles, lay carved lamb in the nest, and pour sauce over.

Tip: Lamb loin is best when sliced on the bias.

Rocky Mountain Grill

A variety of spices combine to give these chops an unforget-table flavor. This recipe is courtesy of the American Lamb Council. 4 to 6 servings.

6 to 8 loin chops, well-trimmed of fat
$1/2$ teaspoon salt
$1/2$ teaspoon pepper
$1/4$ teaspoon cayenne pepper
$1/2$ cup light vegetable oil
3 tablespoons balsamic vinegar
6 leaves fresh sage **or** 1 tablespoon dried
1 tablespoon minced onion
1 teaspoon coarse-grained mustard
1 teaspoon grated lemon peel
$1/4$ teaspoon ground cloves

Sprinkle salt, pepper and cayenne to taste onto both sides of the chops. In a glass or ceramic container, stir together remaining the ingredients. Add chops and marinate in refrigerator for 4 to 24 hours. Stir occasionally.
Broil chops 4 to 6 inches from the source of heat for 6 minutes on each side, or until desired doneness is reached. Brush with marinade at least once on each side.

To grill:
Push coals to either side of the grill and place a drip pan in the center. (This will prevent a fire flare-up). Grill the chops 6 minutes per side, or until desired doneness is reached.

Sunny Lemon Chops

Lemon juice tenderizes lamb and adds a sparkle to the flavor of the meat. A simple green salad and fresh wheat rolls or crusty bread would complete this easy, yet elegant, supper. 4 servings.

8 loin **or** rib lamb chops, 1- to 2-inches-thick, well-trimmed
1 tablespoon lemon-pepper*
2 fresh lemons, cut into quarters
2 tablespoons fresh oregano, minced **or** 1 tablespoon dried

Preheat broiler, or light the barbecue. Season chops with lemon-pepper. Place them on grill and cook to desired doneness. When done, remove to a platter. Squeeze quartered lemons over each chop and sprinkle the oregano over tops.

*Variations:

Substitute *one* of the following for lemon-pepper:
1 tablespoon garlic salt **or** fresh minced garlic
1 tablespoon dried rosemary **or** fresh rosemary, crumbled

Swiss Chops

Swiss cheese lends a nutty flavor to these chops. 4 servings.

4 rib chops, trimmed of excess fat
4 thin onion slices
4 slices Swiss cheese

Broil chops in a preheated broiler for 7 minutes. Turn them over and broil for 5 minutes. Remove from oven and place onion and Swiss cheese on top. Broil for 2 minutes, or until cheese begins to melt.

Garlic Chops

Excellent served with small new potatoes. 2 servings.

2 (6-ounce) lamb chops, trimmed of excess fat
2 teaspoons olive oil
1 whole head garlic, peeled and pressed
1/2 cup canned artichoke bottoms, diced
1/2 cup red wine
1 teaspoon fresh oregano, crumbled

Preheat oven to 350°F. Coat a baking dish with oil, reserving 1 teaspoon. Brush chops lightly with teaspoon of oil. Spread garlic on each chop. Arrange chops in baking dish. Bake for 40 to 50 minutes.

Combine artichoke bottoms, wine and oregano in a small saucepan, bring to a boil and simmer for 15 minutes. Spoon sauce over baked chops.

Variation:
Broil chops over a gas or charcoal barbecue for an even richer flavor.

Lamb in Minted Vinegar Sauce

The Willamette Valley in Oregon is one of the world's major producers of mint. My herb garden is a major producer of both spearmint and peppermint, but I don't mind at all, as mint and lamb go so well together that I use a lot of it. 4 servings.

8 loin lamb chops (each about 1½-inch-thick), trimmed
2 tablespoons green onions, chopped
½ cup balsamic vinegar
2 tablespoons fresh mint **or** 1 tablespoon dried
¼ teaspoon salt
½ teaspoon pepper
1 teaspoon vegetable cooking oil

Combine onions and vinegar in a small saucepan and simmer for 3 minutes, or until syrupy. Remove from heat and stir in mint. Set aside.

Dry chops by blotting with a paper towel, then season them with salt and pepper. Coat skillet with the teaspoon of oil. Sear lamb chops in hot skillet for 4 minutes per side (for medium-well). Vary browning time according to your preference. See chart on page 14.

Strain the vinegar-mint sauce and pour it over the cooked chops.

Lamb Chops with Mint Stuffing

Any type of lamb chops may be used for this zippy dish.
Shoulder chops are the most economical cut. 4 servings.

8 lamb shoulder chops
$1/4$ cup onion, minced
$1/4$ cup celery, minced
2 tablespoons butter **or** margarine
1 cup fresh mint leaves, torn
3 cups stale bread, torn into pieces
1 egg
$1/2$ teaspoon salt
$1/2$ teaspoon pepper

Preheat oven to 350°F. Sauté the onion and celery in the butter. Stir in the mint and bread. Season with salt and pepper. Break the egg into a small bowl and whisk. Stir beaten egg into the bread mixture, until well combined.

Place shoulder chops in a shallow baking dish. Put stuffing mixture on top of lamb chops. Bake in oven for 1 hour.

A Day in Clark Gable's Diet

Movie star, Clark Gable, occasionally dieted to stay fit and trim. Simple broiled lamb chops were a favorite menu item.

Breakfast: $1/2$ Grapefruit & Black Coffee

Lunch: 2 Lamb Chops (broiled)
Lettuce & a Glass of Tomato Juice

Dinner: Squash, Cauliflower & String Beans
Applesauce

Stuffed Lamb Chops with Horseradish Cream Sauce

This can be prepared ahead and reheated in the microwave, while you make the sauce. Serve with the Horseradish Cream Sauce* on the side. 2 servings.

2 (6-ounce) double-boned lamb chops (over 1-inch-thick),
    trimmed of excess fat
1 tablespoon butter **or** margarine
1 tablespoon flour
4 tablespoons chopped fresh mushrooms
1 teaspoon chopped fresh parsley
1/4 teaspoon salt
1/4 teaspoon pepper
1/8 teaspoon Worcestershire sauce
1 egg, beaten
1/2 cup cracker crumbs
1/4 cup vegetable oil

Combine butter and flour until very smooth (this is a roux). Add mushrooms, parsley, seasonings and Worcestershire sauce; mix well. Make an opening between the bones, and stuff chops with mushroom mixture. Dip stuffed chops into beaten egg, then coat with cracker crumbs. Panfry chops in heated vegetable oil about 10 minutes per side, or until golden brown.

*Horseradish Cream Sauce

2 tablespoons butter **or** margarine
2 tablespoons flour
1 cup milk (2% preferred)
2 tablespoons prepared horseradish sauce

Combine the butter and flour in a small saucepan. Heat until bubbling, then slowly add milk, stirring constantly. Cook until thickened, then add horseradish.

Sirloin Lamb Steaks with Spanish Sherry Sauce

This complete meal recipe from the American Sheep Industry Association features a newer lamb cut, lamb sirloin steaks. Sirloin steak is actually a cross-section taken from the first four inches of a full leg of lamb. Steaks can also be cut into shish-kebob cubes, cutlets or thin strips for stir-fry. 6 servings.

2 (1-inch-thick) lamb sirloin steaks (about 1½-pounds)
3 russet potatoes, each cut into 8 wedges
1 red bell pepper, cut into 8 strips
1 green bell pepper, cut into 8 strips
1 yellow bell pepper, cut into 8 strips

Place potato wedges on a paper towel or microwave roasting rack and microwave on HIGH (100%) for 10 to 12 minutes. While potatoes are cooking make sauce.

Broil steaks and vegetables under a broiler, or over a hot barbecue grill for 5 to 6 minutes. Turn and brush with sauce. Cook 2 to 3 minutes longer for medium-rare. Cut steaks into thirds and serve with grilled vegetables.

Spanish Sherry Sauce
Makes 1¼ cups.

½ cup unsweetened apple juice **or** dry sherry
½ cup honey
2 tablespoons tomato paste
2 tablespoons red wine vinegar
2 tablespoons minced onion
1 teaspoon Worcestershire sauce
½ teaspoon freshly ground pepper

In a small saucepan, combine all sauce ingredients. Simmer 5 minutes. Set sauce aside.

Pikes Peak Barbecued Lamb Steaks

Lamb is so succulent when barbecued and this zesty sauce is great. 2 servings.

2 lamb sirloin steaks, 1-inch-thick

Pikes Peak Barbecue Sauce:
¼ cup minced onion
¼ cup minced green pepper
2 teaspoons olive oil
¾ cup chili sauce
¼ cup orange juice
2 tablespoons brown sugar
2 teaspoons grated orange peel (zest)
5 drops red pepper sauce

Sauté onion and green pepper in olive oil for 3 minutes. Add remaining sauce ingredients. Cover and simmer for 10 minutes. Brush sauce onto lamb steaks and grill.

Teriyaki Lamb Steaks

This quick, easy recipe (courtesy of the American Sheep Industry Association) has the flavor of the Far East. 2 servings.

2 lamb sirloin steaks, 1-inch-thick
½ cup soy sauce
1 tablespoon brown sugar
¼ teaspoon ground ginger
¼ teaspoon ground nutmeg
2 tablespoons lemon juice

Arrange steaks in a glass dish. In a small bowl, combine soy sauce, sugar, ginger, nutmeg and lemon juice and pour over lamb. Cover and refrigerate for several hours. Remove from marinade and broil 3- to 4-inches from heat, for 6 to 8 minutes on each side; baste frequently with marinade.

Any Country Quick Shanks

For the busy cook, peeled, diced, canned tomatoes, seasoned with either Italian, Mexican or Cajun spices, are a real blessing. The type you choose sets the tone! This dish is good over toast points. 4 servings.

4 lamb shanks
$1/2$ cup flour
$1/4$ cup light olive **or** vegetable oil
1 (14 $1/2$-ounce) can peeled stewed tomatoes

Dredge shanks in flour; save unused flour to thicken juices. Heat oil in a heavy skillet, or a deep casserole dish. Brown shanks quickly over a high burner. Add tomatoes with juices, cover, and simmer at least 2 hours. Remove shanks from skillet. Thicken juices with reserved flour. Add shanks and continue cooking over low heat for $1 1/2$ hours, or until meat falls off the bones.

"It's been a long life and a hard one, but I always had a bit of lamb to eat with a crust of bread and now and then, a pint of ale. So it was alright, I suppose."

Bridget McManahan
My Simple Life

Garden Shanks

Shanks are like little legs of lamb - and you can allow one per person. This is a delicious slow-cooking way to enjoy them. Just add hot biscuits for a meal to remember. 4 servings.

4 lamb shanks
1 lemon, cut in quarters
$^{1}/_{2}$ cup flour, divided
1 teaspoon lemon pepper
$^{1}/_{4}$ cup light olive oil **or** vegetable oil
1 (10$^{1}/_{2}$-ounce) can condensed, low-sodium beef broth
1 cup water
$^{1}/_{2}$ cup dry vermouth (optional)
1 medium yellow onion, chopped
4 carrots, peeled and cut into chunks
4 stalks of celery, peeled and cut into chunks

Rub each shank with a lemon quarter. Mix the flour (less 2 tablespoons) and lemon pepper together. Dredge shanks in seasoned flour. Heat oil in a heavy skillet or deep casserole dish. Brown shanks quickly over a hot burner.

Pour beef broth over shanks. Cover skillet and simmer slowly over low heat for 2 hours, or until the meat is fork-tender. Add water, as needed, and set aside.

Stir reserved 2 tablespoons of flour into liquid in pan and cook until thickened. Stir in vermouth. Return shanks to gravy and add vegetables. Re-cover skillet and bake in a 350°F oven for 1$^{1}/_{2}$ hours. Remove bones and serve meat with the vegetables and gravy.

Herb-Baked Lamb Shanks

Oven-roasted shanks are tender and full of flavor. Cooking the shanks in foil saves washing a pan. 4 servings.

4 lamb shanks
4 cloves of garlic, peeled and minced
1 teaspoon dried thyme
1 teaspoon dried rosemary
$\frac{1}{2}$ teaspoon salt
1 teaspoon white pepper
4 tablespoons tomato purée
1 cup dry red wine (a Merlot works well)

Preheat oven to 325°F. Place each shank on an 18-inch square of heavy oven foil. Put a minced garlic clove over each; sprinkle with remaining herbs and seasonings.

Shape foil around shanks, leaving the top open. Pour 1 tablespoon tomato purée over each shank and pour $\frac{1}{4}$ cup of wine into the foil. Seal foil around shanks tightly. Place the foil-wrapped shanks in a baking dish and bake for two hours, or until very tender.

Rice-Stuffed Shanks

This is a recipe my mother made for company. Stuffing the shanks is easier than it sounds, as there are lots of nooks and crannies for the rice. 6 servings.

6 lamb shanks
2 tablespoons light vegetable oil
2 cups water
1 teaspoon salt
1 teaspoon pepper
1 teaspoon dried rosemary
1 cup raw white rice
2 cups low-sodium beef broth
2 tablespoons cornstarch
1/4 cup water

Heat oil in a heavy skillet and brown shanks. Turn frequently for even cooking. Pour water and seasonings over. Reduce heat, cover, and simmer for 1½ hours, or until fork-tender. Remove shanks, leaving juices.

Cook rice in beef broth, let cool. Stuff shanks with the cooked rice. Place stuffed shanks in a kettle or Dutch oven.

Combine cornstarch with cool water and add to juices. Stir frequently, until thickened. Pour gravy over shanks, cover, and cook over medium heat for ½ hour.

Sweet & Sour Shanks

This is a delicious way to liven up lamb. It's good served with brown rice. 4 servings.

4 lamb shanks
4 tablespoons flour
2 tablespoons light vegetable oil
1 teaspoon salt
1 teaspoon pepper
1 chicken bouillon cube
2 cups boiling water
1 garlic clove, minced
1 bay leaf
4 whole cloves
1 teaspoon Worcestershire sauce
1/4 cup cider vinegar
2 tablespoons brown sugar
1/2 teaspoon dry mustard
1 onion, peeled and chopped

Roll shanks in flour. Heat oil in a skillet and brown shanks. Sprinkle with salt and pepper.

Dissolve bouillon cube in boiling water and slowly pour over the shanks. Add remaining spices, herbs and onion. Cover and simmer for 1 1/2 hours, or until fork-tender.

Vino Shanks – Microwaved!

Need dinner in a hurry? Cook this flavorful meal in your microwave oven. Expect it to become a favorite recipe. 4 servings.

4 lamb shanks
1 cup onion, sliced
2 cups peeled and sliced carrots
1¹/₂ cups chopped celery
1 teaspoon salt
1 teaspoon pepper
1 bay leaf
2 tablespoons flour
¹/₂ cup water
¹/₂ cup red wine

In a 2¹/₂-quart or larger microwave-safe casserole, combine lamb shanks, onion, celery, carrots, seasonings and bay leaf.

Mix flour with water until dissolved; add wine. Pour this sauce over shanks and vegetables. Cover and cook on HIGH (100% power) for 28 minutes. Turn the shanks at least three times to coat them evenly with the wine sauce. Let stand, covered, for 15 minutes to finish cooking.

Nomadic sheepherders in the Near East first began roasting skewered pieces of lamb or mutton over their campfires. This simple form of barbecued meat became known as Shish Kebab (or Kabob). The name comes from the Turkish word, *shish*, which means skewer, and *kebap* meaning roast meat.

Today, this term means almost any combination of meat, vegetables or fruit cooked on a skewer.

Barbecued Lamb

Barbecued Lamb

The Cossacks - an ethnic breed of wandering soldiers, almost mercenaries - who roamed the steppes of Eastern and Central Russia on horseback, depended on their speed and lightness of travel for success. If they came upon a mature sheep as they rode, they would fillet the meat and lay the pieces under the saddle blanket and ride all day. When they stopped for the night, the mutton was tenderized and seasoned with salt from the horses' sweat. They would only have to thread the meat onto sticks and roast it over an open fire.

Today's cook has only to light a match on the grill to enjoy similar flavors. Grilling meat is also another way to reduce fats– the fat will drip away onto the coals below.

Many kitchens have grills built-in for outdoor barbecued flavor the year around. A wide variety of coals and wood flavors add to the enjoyment. Lamb lends itself well to grilling. The Cossacks knew a good thing when they saw it!

Keith Kabobs

Mike Hedman, Pilot Rock, Oregon, won Grand Prize and First Place in the Oregon Sheep Growers' 1992 Lamb Cook-Off barbecue category with these fresh vegetable and lamb kabobs. You have to admit, Oregonians have a way with lamb! Just add steamed couscous or a rice pilaf for a great healthy meal. 6 servings.

1½ pounds boneless lamb, cut into 1½-inch cubes
1 cup onion, cut in quarters (1 large onion)
1 cup green pepper, cut into 1-inch pieces (1 pepper)
1 pound mushrooms, washed
1 cup zucchini, cut into ½-inch pieces, (about 1 zucchini)
1 cup light Italian salad dressing

Trim meat of excess fat. Place meat in a bowl and add salad dressing, cover. Refrigerate 4 to 8 hours; turn meat occasionally.

Place meat on barbecue skewers, alternating with onion, pepper, mushroom and zucchini.

Cook kabobs over medium coals for 10 to 15 minutes. Turn kabobs every 3 minutes and coat with dressing. Brush with additional dressing with each turning.

Sweet & Sour Kabobs

The taste of the tropics comes through on these Kabobs.
Excellent alongside baked yams or Chinese fried rice.
6 servings.

2 pounds lean lamb, trimmed of fat and cut into 2-inch cubes
1 (8-ounce) can pineapple chunks
2 green peppers, cut into 2-inch chunks

Marinade:
$^{1}/_{2}$ cup vinegar
$^{1}/_{2}$ cup vegetable oil
$^{1}/_{2}$ teaspoon salt
$^{1}/_{4}$ teaspoon pepper
$^{1}/_{4}$ cup fresh mint, crushed*
$^{1}/_{2}$ cup pineapple juice

Combine all ingredients. Marinate lamb chunks at least 2 hours.

Thread lamb, alternating it with pineapple chunks and peppers, on skewers. Place skewers over a medium fire for 20 minutes. Turn over, baste with the marinade and cook for another 20 minutes.

*Note: Use a mortar and pestle to crush the mint. If you are out in the woods camping, a heavy small bowl and a clean rock will do just as well!

Hickory Pocket Lamb Chops

This 1991 Grand Prize winner of the 1st Oregon Lamb Cook-Off, held in Heppner, Oregon, is sure to be a winner in your book, too! 3 to 6 servings.

6 (1-inch-thick) lamb chops
Red wine
1 (8-ounce) can hickory smoke flavored almonds
hickory smoke salt to taste

Slice a pocket in the middle of each chop. Marinate chops 8 to 10 hours or overnight in enough red wine to cover.

Chop almonds in a food processor or blender. Put 1 tablespoon chopped almonds into each pocket and sprinkle with salt. Grill 5 to 7 minutes on each side for medium-rare chops.

Lamb Chops with Tangy Mustard Sauce

A zesty and easy lamb chop recipe shared by the Weber Company, makers of excellent outdoor kettle barbecues. 4 servings.

8 loin chops, 1-inch-thick, trimmed of excess fat
$1/2$ cup sour cream
4 teaspoons Dijon-style mustard
1 clove garlic, minced

Combine sour cream, mustard and garlic. Set aside. Place chops on a hot charcoal grill 7 to 9 minutes for rare (140°F), 10 to 13 minutes for medium (150°F), or 14 to 17 minutes for medium-well (160-170 °F). Turn chops once, about halfway through the grilling time. Serve with reserved sauce on the side.

Hans' Sure-Fire
Barbecued Loin of Lamb

*Our dear friend, Hans Arenz, is a barbecue expert. He says,
"Because of camping and surprising friends with pies, roasts
and other culinary delights, I developed an avid interest in
barbecuing." The secret to his tender lamb loin recipe is
Mesquite coals. Serves 6 delighted and surprised friends.*

1 (3-pound) loin roast, boned and trimmed of excess fat
2 tablespoons salt
4 garlic cloves, pressed
$1/2$ cup fresh mint, minced
1 tablespoon dried rosemary

Start barbecue coals. Bring the loin to room temperature.
Sprinkle it with salt and press crushed garlic into both sides.
With fork tines, encrust meat with herbs.

Use heavy-duty foil to make a 'tray' large enough to hold
the loin. Spread coals to either side of the barbecue kettle.
Place foil pan in the center of grill. Put lid on kettle with the
vents open.

Roast for 15 to 20 minutes per pound for medium-rare,
longer for more well-done lamb. Do not turn roast over. Let
meat 'rest' for 15 minutes before carving against the grain,
London broil-style.

Parsley-Coated Rack of Lamb

Parsley has a distinctive flavor that is subtle, but very sharp when fresh. I prefer old-fashioned curly parsley, but the newer Italian one is good for this recipe from the Weber Company. 4 servings.

1 (2$\frac{1}{2}$- to 3-pound) lamb rib roast (8 ribs)
1 tablespoon Dijon-style mustard
1 cup soft bread crumbs
$\frac{1}{4}$ cup snipped fresh parsley **or** 4 teaspoons dried
$\frac{1}{4}$ teaspoon salt
$\frac{1}{4}$ teaspoon pepper
2 tablespoons butter **or** margarine, melted
1 clove garlic, minced

Trim excess fat from roast. Spread mustard over lamb and place, rib side up, in a 9 x13-inch metal baking pan.

Combine bread crumbs, parsley, salt and pepper. Stir in melted butter and garlic. Pat mixture onto the meaty side of roast.

Place pan in center of cooking grill. Cover and cook for 1 to 1$\frac{1}{4}$ hours for rare, 1$\frac{1}{4}$ to 1$\frac{1}{2}$ hours for medium and 1$\frac{1}{2}$ hours to 1$\frac{3}{4}$ hours for medium-well. Let roast stand for 15 minutes before carving.

Bonnie's Lamb

*An interesting and creamy marinade made this recipe the
barbecue division winner in 1991 in the Oregon Lamb
Council's Cook-Off. Serve with foil-wrapped baking potatoes
roasted in the hot coals. Turn occasionally. 6 servings.*

1 (5- to 6-pound) leg of lamb, boned and butterflied
1 cup sour cream **or** low-fat yogurt
2 teaspoons MSG (optional)
1 teaspoon salt
$1/4$ teaspoon coarsely cracked black pepper
$1/8$ teaspoon dried oregano
$1/8$ teaspoon dried parsley
$1/8$ teaspoon garlic powder

Trim away the fell (see the glossary, page 10) and fat from
the meat. Combine the sour cream with all the remaining
ingredients. Spread the sour cream marinade thickly on both
sides.

Cover and marinate in refrigerator at least 4 to 5 hours, or
overnight.

Grill over a hot coal fire 20 minutes on each side for
medium-rare meat. Cook an additional 10 minutes for
medium-well done.

"Be as gentle and sweet as a
young lamb's meat."
Constance D'Ambriere

Skewered Leg of Lamb

Nothing tastes better than a leg of lamb on the barbecue. This recipe from the Weber Company is a delightful herb-barbecued entrée that will entrance your guests. Serve with a salad of fresh picked greens from your garden. Serves up to 16 hungry guests.

1 (4- to 5-pound) leg of lamb, boned and butterflied
1 cup Dijon-style mustard
$1/2$ cup light vegetable oil
2 tablespoons dry red wine
2 cloves garlic, crushed
1 teaspoon dried rosemary
1 teaspoon dried basil
$1/2$ teaspoon dried oregano
$1/2$ teaspoon dried thyme
$1/4$ teaspoon pepper

Combine mustard, oil, wine, garlic, rosemary, basil, oregano, thyme and pepper, set aside. Remove the fell (see glossary, page 10) from outer surface of lamb, and trim excess fat. Place lamb in a shallow dish and spread with mustard mixture. Cover and refrigerate for 4 to 8 hours.

Drain lamb, and reserve marinade. Thread two 12-inch skewers through the meat, criss-crossing diagonally. Place lamb in the center of the cooking grill, cover. Grill 45 to 55 minutes for rare, 55 to 65 minutes for medium and 1 to $1^1/4$ hours for medium-well. Brush lamb with marinade during the last 10 minutes of grilling time.

Note: Fresh herbs, if available, may be substituted for the dried. I like to be on the generous side when measuring fresh herbs.

Whiskey-Glazed Leg of Lamb

Shelly Rietmann of Ione, Oregon, took Second Place honors at the Oregon Lamb Council's 1992 Lamb Cook-Off with this unusual recipe. Try it - it's sure to be the talk of the party!
4 to 6 servings.

1 (4- to 6-pound) leg of lamb, trimmed of excess fat

Glaze:
$1/2$ cup butter
$1/3$ cup light vegetable oil
1 garlic clove, minced
$1/2$ cup minced onion
$1/2$ cup whiskey
$1/2$ cup orange juice with pulp
$1/4$ cup maple syrup
4 tablespoons dark molasses
2 tablespoons soy sauce
1 tablespoon ginger
1 teaspoon salt
1 teaspoon pepper
1 tablespoon grated orange peel
3 tablespoons cornstarch

Melt butter over low heat in a large saucepan. Add oil, onion and garlic and sauté until golden. Turn heat up to medium and add the remaining ingredients, *except orange peel and cornstarch.*

Gradually add cornstarch, stirring constantly, until mixture reaches a glaze consistency. Add orange peel and set aside. Generously brush glaze over all sides of the lamb. Cook over a hot barbecue for 40 minutes for medium-rare meat, turning the lamb frequently and brushing additional glaze with each turning. Cook 10 minutes longer for medium-well done.

Herb & Spice Marinade

My fresh marinade recipe is easy to make and always gathers compliments. It can be used with any recipe calling for a marinade. Create your own special variation by changing the herbs and spices. Makes 2 1/2 to 3 cups.

1 cup olive oil
2 medium onions, peeled and minced
6 cloves garlic, peeled and chopped
1 piece fresh ginger-root (about 1 x 2-inches), peeled and chopped
1/2 cup red wine vinegar
1/4 cup sugar
1/2 cup lemon juice

Herbs & Spices:
1 teaspoon fresh rosemary, crumbled
1/2 teaspoon ground cloves
1/4 teaspoon grated fresh nutmeg*
1/4 teaspoon ground cinnamon
1/4 teaspoon ground mace
1 teaspoon cayenne pepper

Combine all ingredients. Pour amount needed to cover lamb. Cover, refrigerate and marinate 12 to 24 hours for best results. Turn meat frequently. Remove lamb from marinade and cook as desired.

* Note: Ground nutmeg may be used. My preference, however, is fresh grated nutmeg which has so much more aroma and flavor.

*If you haven't discovered a little gem of a book called **Easy Microwave Preserving**,* I urge you to rush out and get it at your nearest bookstore. It's a wealth of quick and easy things to do with your microwave oven. I discovered this recipe in the book and it's a favorite around here. Try it on lamb ribs for a country-style feast!*

Fruity Barbecue Sauce

Fresh summer fruits add a special taste to this succulent sauce. Great on ribs! Can be made with apricots, papayas, peaches, pears, or nectarines. Makes about 3 half-pints.

$^1/_4$ cup chopped onion
3 cups peeled and sliced fruit**
$^1/_2$ cup sherry
$^2/_3$ cup packed dark brown sugar
$^2/_3$ cup chili sauce **or** catsup
$^1/_4$ cup cider, fruit **or** white wine vinegar
2 teaspoons dry mustard
1 teaspoon Worcestershire sauce
1 tablespoon molasses
$^1/_2$ teaspoon Tabasco sauce
$^1/_2$ teaspoon salt

Place onion in food processor or blender; process until finely chopped. Add fruit and process until puréed.

Combine all ingredients in a 3-quart (or larger) microwave-safe bowl. Stir. Cover bowl with plastic wrap, leaving vent. Microwave on HIGH (100% power) for 9 to10 minutes, or until mixture reaches a boil. Stir, reduce power to MEDIUM (50%), and microwave for 15 minutes, uncovered, stirring every 5 minutes. Ladle into sterile containers.

•For immediate use: Pour into sterile jars or containers. Keeps several weeks refrigerated.

•For longer storage: Let sauce cool slightly before ladling into freezer containers. Seal. Keeps 6 to 8 months frozen.

**If fresh fruit is out of season, frozen or canned fruit may be substituted. Fruit that is unsweetened or packed in natural juice is preferable.

Variation:

Rhubarb Barbecue Sauce

Substitute 3 cups chopped rhubarb for other fruit. Increase brown sugar to 1 cup packed. Place rhubarb in a 3-quart or larger microwave-safe bowl and microwave on HIGH for 5 to 6 minutes, or until tender. Purée rhubarb with finely chopped onion, and proceed as directed.

Note: Sauce may be prepared conventionally, if preferred. Bring to a beginning boil, stirring constantly, then reduce heat and simmer gently. Stir often until mixture is slightly thickened. Proceed as directed.

*Reprinted with permission from <u>EASY MICROWAVE PRESERVING</u>, ©1992 by Cynthia Fischborn & Cheryl Long, published by The Globe Pequot Press, Old Saybrook, CT 06475.

'Lamb is just like a trip to the ocean. Everyone enjoys something new and different, but the ocean beaches and lamb are at their best when Hot!'

Anon.

Soups, Stews
& Casseroles

Casserole of Eggplant & Lamb

Eggplant has a natural affinity for lamb. This simple casserole proves it. Serve with a warm crusty bread. 6 servings.

3 pounds lamb stew meat, cut into 1-inch cubes
$1/3$ cup olive oil
2 cups peeled and chopped onions (2 large onions)
1 large green bell pepper, trimmed, seeded and chopped
2 eggplants, trimmed and cut into 1-inch cubes
2 cloves garlic, chopped
1 teaspoon cumin
$1/2$ teaspoon fresh grated **or** ground nutmeg
$1^1/2$ teaspoons ground cloves
$1/2$ teaspoon salt
$1/4$ teaspoon pepper
$1/2$ cup white vinegar
2 cups chicken broth
1 cup bread crumbs

Heat oil in a deep ovenproof kettle. Brown lamb in the hot oil. Remove browned meat and add onion and green pepper, stir and cook until golden and soft. Remove from oil and add eggplant. Stir and cook for 5 minutes.

Preheat oven to 350° F. Place lamb, vegetables, spices, vinegar and broth into kettle. Bring to a boil then remove from heat. Sprinkle bread crumbs over top, cover and bake in oven for 1 hour. Remove the cover to allow bread crumbs to brown for the last 15 minutes.

Lamb in Suitcases

My mother was nothing, if not inventive. Faced with a summer garden that got out of hand and some ground lamb, which we always seemed to have in the freezer, she would simply combine it all into something tasty. This was a favorite. 6 servings.

1½ pounds ground lamb
¾ cup raw rice
1 teaspoon salt
½ teaspoon pepper
1 teaspoon allspice
½ cup tomato paste, thinned with 2 tablespoons water
12 summer squash **or** 4 small eggplants **or** 6 medium
  zucchini squash
2 tablespoons lemon juice
1 garlic clove, crushed
3 ripe tomatoes, chopped
2 tablespoons fresh mint, washed and chopped
Parmesan cheese, freshly grated

Preheat oven to 350°F. Mix lamb, rice, seasonings and tomato paste together. Wash vegetables and remove stems. Scoop out insides to make cases. Fill vegetable cases with lamb mixture. Stand cases upright or lay them in a deep baking dish. Mix lemon juice, garlic, tomatoes and mint together. Spoon mixture over tops of cases. Fill dish with water to cover the bottom half of the vegetable cases (this prevents scorching and steams the vegetables).

Bake for 1 hour. Just before serving, sprinkle freshly grated Parmesan cheese over tops of the cases.

Herbed Lamb in Sour Cream

I am always fascinated by what other people invent, and this recipe is no exception. Barbara Smallwood, a native of the high desert town of Bend, Oregon, developed this recipe for an Oregon Lamb Cook-off. Her use of caraway seeds adds an unusual "bite" to the flavor that I like. Serve over a bed of white or brown rice or egg noodles. 4 servings.

1 ½ pounds lean lamb, cut into ½-inch cubes
¼ cup flour
2 teaspoons salt
½ teaspoon pepper
1 teaspoon tarragon
½ teaspoon thyme
2 tablespoons butter **or** margarine
1 ½ cups chicken stock
1 teaspoon caraway seeds
¼ cup lemon juice
1 cup sour cream
2 tablespoons white wine

Mix flour, salt, pepper, tarragon and thyme. Dredge lamb cubes in the seasoned flour to coat.

Melt butter in a frying pan and brown the meat. Pour chicken broth over and stir in caraway seeds, lemon juice, sour cream and wine. Mix well, cover and cook over a very low heat for 1 ½ hours.

Persian Lamb With Peaches

Phyllis Potts, award-winning author of **Going Against the Grain: Wheat-Free Cookery** *(Central Point Publishing), shares her wonderfully spiced and fruited lamb dish. Serve over rice and garnish with yogurt and fresh mint leaves. 4 to 6 servings.*

2 pounds lean boneless lamb shoulder
1 teaspoon ground cinnamon
¹/₂ teaspoon ground cloves
¹/₄ teaspoon salt **or** to taste
¹/₂ teaspoon pepper
2 tablespoons brown sugar
1 medium onion, peeled and chopped
3 tablespoons lemon juice, divided
4 teaspoons cornstarch
4 teaspoons water
1 pound peaches **or** nectarines **or** pears, peeled and sliced
Sprigs of fresh mint, washed and patted dry

Trim excess fat from lamb and cut into ³/₄-inch cubes. Arrange lamb in shallow 2-quart baking dish. In a small bowl, combine cinnamon, cloves, salt, pepper and brown sugar. Sprinkle mixture over lamb and top with onions and 2 tablespoons of the lemon juice.

Cover baking dish with plastic wrap. Microwave on HIGH (100% power) for 5 minutes, stir. Microwave on MEDIUM (50% power) for 30 minutes, or until meat is fork tender, stirring half-way through cooking time. Let stand 5 minutes. Remove lamb to a platter and cover.

Mix cornstarch and water until smooth and stir into lamb juices. Microwave on HIGH for 2 to 3 minutes, stirring every minute until thickened. Add reserved lamb to sauce. Arrange sliced peaches on lamb, sprinkle with remaining lemon juice and garnish with mint.

Irish Stews–Ancient & Modern

When my friend, Michael, left for Ireland to get his doctorate in Gaelic, I asked him to send me some authentic Irish recipes. He wrote back a few months later and said that he met an old crone near Galway Bay who gave him this recipe which had been in her family for some time. She spoke in Gaelic, the lilting language of the Emerald Isles, as old as the hills themselves. Michael translated it, and sent it off to me.

"This takes about two hours. Cut up the lamb into small pieces–say about two inches square. Use the loin if you can. If you can't, it will still be good.

Wash it and put it over the fire in a stew pan. Put layers of potatoes, turnips and onions–cut all smallish–in with the meat. Salt pork, if you have it, adds to the flavor, you know. If you don't have it, then don't worry.

Now you put in cold water, say a pitcher-full. Cover this pot closely and stew it gently now until all the vegetables are ready to mash and the greater part of the gravy is gone into the vegetables. Put this into a bowl and serve it hot with dumplings, if you have the flour. If you don't, it will be alright. It's very filling."

Translation Irish Stew

Bringing this recipe up to date was easy. Just listen to what the wise old woman had to say. 8 servings.

3 pounds lamb stew meat (loin preferred)
2 tablespoons vegetable oil
2 cups coarsely chopped onions
6 potatoes, peeled and cut into 2-inch cubes
2 turnips, peeled and cut into 2-inch cubes
1 ½ cups boiling water
1 teaspoon salt
½ teaspoon white pepper
2 whole cloves
2 tablespoons flour (approximately)

Cut lamb into cubes and remove any fat or membranes. Heat oil in a heavy deep skillet or Dutch oven. Add lamb and brown well, turning frequently. Add onions, potatoes and turnips along with boiling water and spices. Cover and simmer for 2 hours, adding more water, if necessary.

Remove cloves. Pour liquid from skillet into a large measuring cup. Measure liquid. For each cup of stock, use 1 tablespoon flour. Pour liquid into a large saucepan and bring to a boil. Cook and stir constantly, until thickened. Pour the gravy back into the skillet and heat the stew through. Adjust seasonings, if necessary.

Variation:
¼ cup diced salt pork may be added. Sauté in skillet first and omit vegetable oil. Continue as directed.

Lamb Stew in a Puff Bowl

Another great recipe from lamb country that is a complete meal-in-a-dish! Jim Boor won First Place in conventional cooking with this recipe in the 1993 Oregon Sheep Growers Association Lamb Cook-Off. 4 to 6 servings.

Stew:

2 pounds cubed lamb stew meat
2 tablespoons vegetable oil
1 (8-ounce) can green beans
2 (8-ounce) cans tomato sauce
4 potatoes, peeled and cubed
1 teaspoon Tabasco sauce
1 teaspoon salt
$^1/_2$ teaspoon pepper

Preheat oven to 350°F. In a heavy pan, brown stew meat in oil, until browned. Combine lamb with all the remaining ingredients in a 2-quart casserole dish. Bake for 1 hour.

Puff Bowl:

$^2/_3$ cup water
$^1/_4$ cup butter **or** margarine
1 cup baking mix
4 eggs

Preheat oven to 400°F. Boil water and butter in a medium saucepan. Add baking mix and stir vigorously over low heat until a ball forms, about 1 to 2 minutes. Remove from heat. Beat in 1 egg at a time, until smooth. Spread dough in a greased 9-inch pie plate. (Do not spread up the sides of the plate). Bake at 400 degrees F, until the center is dry: about 35 minutes. Remove from oven and fill with stew.

Lamb with Rubies & Emeralds

This is so simple to do, it is almost embarrassing. Served with pasta and crusty rolls, it will be a favorite with your family, too. Just don't tell them how easy it is. 4 servings.

1 pound shoulder lamb meat, trimmed of excess fat and cut into 1-inch cubes
1 medium onion, chopped
1 (20-ounce) can whole tomatoes with juice
$1/2$ teaspoon parsley
$1/2$ teaspoon salt
$1/4$ teaspoon pepper
1 pound fresh trimmed green beans **or** (8-ounce) package of frozen French-style green beans

Sauté meat until the pinkness is gone. Remove from pan with a slotted spoon. Sauté onion in the leftover fat until it is transparent. Add tomatoes, seasonings and meat. Reduce heat, and simmer on low for 1 hour. Add green beans and continue to cook for an additional 10 minutes.

'To separate the sheep from the goats meant that goats were once thought to be in league with the devil.'
Morris Dictionary
of Words and Phrase Origins

Lamb Stew on the Fast Track

Here is a fast, easy and nutritious way to prepare lamb stew using your microwave oven. 4 servings.

1 pound lamb stew meat, cut into 1-inch cubes
1 (³/₄ to 1 ¹/₄-ounce) package of instant brown gravy mix
¹/₂ teaspoon sugar
2 tablespoons flour
1 clove garlic, minced
1 teaspoon Worcestershire sauce
¹/₂ cup red wine*
1 cup water
3 medium-sized carrots, cubed
1 stalk of celery, chopped
¹/₂ white onion, chopped
2 large red potatoes, cubed
1 teaspoon salt
¹/₂ teaspoon pepper

In a large microwave-safe casserole, combine the lamb, gravy mix and sugar. Cook, uncovered, for 5 minutes on HIGH (100%). Stir in the remaining ingredients and cook, covered, for 20 minutes on HIGH, or until the meat and vegetables are done. Stir occasionally.

*Note: If wine is omitted, increase water by ¹/₂ cup.

Moroccan Lamb Stew

Sometimes men who don't usually cook come up with the most amazing and delicious recipes. Perhaps this is because no one ever told them that certain things simply won't work; they just go ahead and do what they think sounds good. This is the case with a friend, a bachelor, who loves to cook and loves lamb, in that order. This unusual dish can be frozen and reheated later. It actually improves with age! Serve over Daffodil Rice (page 118). It is a wonderful company dish. 6 servings.

3 pounds boneless lamb stew meat, trimmed of excess fat
1 cup whole blanched almonds
2 tablespoons almond oil
2 cups chopped onion
2 cloves garlic, minced
1 teaspoon ground cumin
1 teaspoon ground ginger
1 teaspoon salt
1 cinnamon stick
1 can undiluted beef broth
1/4 cup chopped fresh parsley **or** 1/3 cup dried parsley
1 cup pitted chopped dates
1 tablespoon honey

Brown almonds in a 350°F oven by spreading them on a cookie sheet for 5 to 10 minutes. Watch carefully to keep them from burning. Brown lamb in almond oil in a heavy pot with a lid. Remove meat with a slotted spoon and add garlic and onions to the oil. Cook and stir, until soft. Return meat to pot and add cumin, ginger, salt, cinnamon stick and beef broth. Bring to a boil and simmer gently, uncovered, for 1 1/2 hours. Stir in toasted almonds, parsley, dates and honey. Cover the pot and let it 'sit' or 'rest' for 1/2 hour, before serving.

Most Happy Lamb

The Chinese believe that lamb gives heat to the body. On a cold winter night, this braised lamb would heat up anyone. Ideal served with stir-fried Chinese greens and steamed rice. 6 servings.

3 pounds lean lamb, cut into 2-inch cubes
1 cup turnips, cut into 1-inch cubes
2 tablespoons vegetable oil
$1/2$ cup green onions, chopped
1 slice ginger, diced (approximately $1/4$ cup)
1 tablespoon sherry
$1/2$ teaspoon salt
6 tablespoons soy sauce
1 cup boiling water
1 tablespoon sugar

Bring a pot of water to a boil and boil lamb and turnips separately for 5 minutes each. Drain and discard the water.

Heat oil in a wok or heavy skillet and stir-fry the green onion and ginger for 1 minute. Add the lamb, sherry, salt, soy sauce and boiling water. Bring to a boil, stirring, until thick. Cover and simmer $1 1/2$ hours, stirring occasionally to prevent burning. Add turnips and sugar. Bring to a boil and simmer for 20 minutes.

Scotch Soup

The Scots, whom I proudly claim in my family tree, are great keepers of sheep. They use the wool for their famous tartans and eat the meat of the older ewes- those no longer able to raise lambs - a very thrifty practice. Barley is a staple grain in Scotland, and the two team up for what some people call, "a Scotch Broth." My soup is a meal in itself. Add an oat bread and green salad, if you wish. 8 servings.

2 pounds lamb shoulder meat, cut into 2-inch pieces
$1/2$ cup pearl barley, soaked 12 hours, drained
8 cups cold water, reserve $1/4$ cup
2 tablespoons butter **or** margarine
$1/2$ cup peeled diced turnips
$1/2$ cup peeled diced carrots
$3/4$ cup peeled diced tomatoes
$1/2$ cup white onion, diced
3 tablespoons cornstarch
1 teaspoon salt
$1/2$ teaspoon pepper

Add lamb and barley to cold water and bring up to a beginning boil. Reduce heat and simmer for 2 hours, or until meat is very tender.

Sauté vegetables in butter for 5 minutes. Add vegetables to the lamb and simmer for another 30 minutes. Stir cornstarch into reserved $1/4$ cup water. Pour mixture slowly into hot soup, stirring constantly. After soup thickens, add seasonings and adjust to taste.

White Stew

Another popular stew from Ireland. Simple to prepare, it is a welcome change from the heavier 'brown' stews. Try this with my Nearly Irish Bread (page 123). 6 servings.

3 pounds lamb stew meat, cut into 1-inch cubes
2 tablespoons flour
¹/₄ cup vegetable shortening
2 cups water
¹/₂ cup dry white wine
6 medium potatoes, peeled and cut into quarters
  (about 5 cups)
4 medium onions, chopped
1 teaspoon dried thyme
¹/₄ teaspoon pepper
¹/₄ teaspoon salt

Preheat oven to 325°F. In a heavy pot that can go into the oven, melt shortening. Dredge lamb in flour and brown in pot. Add water, wine and vegetables, then add seasonings. Cover pot with a tight fitting lid and bake stew for 2¹/₂ hours.

Zorba's Dilly Lamb Stew

The Greeks, as well as the Scandinavians, know that dill is an herb that loves lamb. Dillkot Pa Lamm is a favorite dish in the land of ice and snow. Dill is also the herb of ancient Egypt. In the British Isles during the Middle Ages, dill was used to repel witches. This is a dilly of a dish! 6 servings.

3 pounds of lamb stew meat, cut into 1-inch cubes
1 teaspoon salt
1 teaspoon pepper
$^1/_2$ cup olive oil
$^1/_2$ cup water (add more if needed)
2 cups of fresh dill, chopped **or** 1 cup, dried
8 green onions, chopped
$^3/_4$ cup lemon juice
2 teaspoons sugar
French bread

Heat olive oil in a large casserole. Brown lamb on all sides, stirring often. Sprinkle with salt and pepper. Add water to pan, reduce heat, cover tightly and simmer, until the meat is fork-tender: about 1 hour. Add more water, if necessary.

Add dill, onion, lemon juice and sugar. Bring up to a boil. Adjust seasonings and serve with a thick slice of French bread at the bottom of soup bowl.

Stews

Wallis Warfield Simpson's Lamb

We can close our eyes and imagine we are guests at the wedding of the century - the marriage of the Duke of Windsor and Wallis Warfield Spencer Simpson. Most of us have heard the story of the then King Edward VIII of England giving up his throne for "the woman he loved".

It is a sunny day, Thursday, June 3, 1937. The time is 10:30 in the morning. You are standing outside a fairy-tale castle in France. Suddenly, the royal couple appears on the balcony! She is slim and wears a long simple gown in a color that will come to be known forever-after as, 'Wallis Blue'. He looks terribly British. And happy.

Imagine being one of only 16 guests chosen by the newly-wed couple to enjoy a wedding breakfast, served buffet-style. The menu was chosen by Wallis herself, and reflects a bit of the personality and charm that captivated the Prince of Wales. It is both elegant and simple, a description that fits the new Duchess of Windsor. The menu, which combined American and British foods, created a sensation at the time for its innovative cuisine reflecting the two countries tastes.

MENU

Creamed Chicken à la Duchesse	*Strawberries*
Baked Ham	*Old Dominion Wedding Cake*
Burgundy Lamb Stew (pg. 85)	*with Buttercream Frosting*
Baked Herbed Rice	*Champagne*
Tossed Green Salad	*Earl Grey Tea*
French Bread	*Coffee*

Burgundy Lamb Stew

This is the recipe for the stew that Wallis served. The hearty flavor of Burgundy wine makes this a stew that warms one's insides on a winter's night. And it is so romantic! 6 servings.

3 pounds lean lamb, cut into 1-inch cubes
½ cup olive oil
2 cups chopped onions
1 teaspoon garlic purée
1 cup flour
3 cups beef broth
1½ cups dry Burgundy or other red wine
1 tablespoon Worcestershire sauce
1 (6-ounce) can tomato paste
1 teaspoon salt
1 teaspoon pepper
1 teaspoon thyme
1 bay leaf
2 cups carrots, peeled and sliced ½-inch thick
1 package (8-ounces) frozen petite peas

Heat oil in a heavy pot. Brown meat. Remove meat from pot and add onions. Stir and cook, until tender, but not brown. Stir in garlic and then the flour. Stir, until lump-free. Add the stock, wine, Worcestershire sauce, tomato paste and seasonings. Bring to a simmer, then cover and cook over low heat for 30 minutes. Add carrots and potatoes and cook an additional 30 to 40 minutes. Adjust seasonings and stir in peas. Cook at a simmer for 5 minutes longer and serve.

'A friendly swarry*, consisting of a boiled leg of mutton with the usual trimmings.'

Dickens, Pickwick Papers,
*old English word for 'meal'

Ground & Variety Lamb

Black Bean Lamb Chili

This chili dish is often requested by my friends. They love it because it's different, and I like it because it's easy to make. 6 servings.

1½ pounds ground lamb
1 cup chopped onion
2 (14-ounce) cans whole tomatoes with juice
1 cup dry red wine (optional)
1 tablespoon chili powder
1 tablespoon fresh oregano, crushed
1 teaspoon sugar
½ teaspoon salt
2 garlic cloves, peeled and minced
2 (15-ounce) cans black beans, drained

Brown lamb in a heavy skillet. Add onion and stir, until the onion is transparent and meat crumbled. Drain off excess fat. Add tomatoes with juice, wine, spices, herbs and garlic. Bring to a boil. Reduce heat, stir and cover. Simmer for 2 hours. Add black beans, cover, and simmer for an additional 30 minutes.

Curry in a Hurry

This was viewed with some skepticism by a friend who I asked over as a guinea pig for my new lamb creation. Perhaps it was the name? In any case, he not only asked for seconds, he asked for the recipe. Serve this curried lamb loaf with rice and a chutney (see pages 110 to 112). 6 servings.

2 pounds ground lamb
2 tablespoons cooking oil
4 tablespoons butter **or** margarine
2 medium apples, cored, quartered and diced
2 medium onions, peeled and sliced
1¹/₂ tablespoons curry powder*
¹/₄ cup chopped almonds
¹/₄ cup raisins
¹/₄ teaspoon salt
¹/₈ teaspoon pepper
4 tablespoons fresh lemon juice
1 cup bread crumbs
2 large eggs, beaten
Chutney for accompaniment

Preheat oven to 350°F. Heat oil in a large skillet and brown ground lamb for 10 minutes, stirring often. Drain off all but 1 tablespoon fat. Place meat into a mixing bowl and set aside. Melt butter in the pan and sauté the apples, onions, curry powder, almonds and raisins. Add seasonings and lemon juice. Add reserved meat, cover and cook for 5 minutes. Stir in bread crumbs and eggs. Press mixture into a loaf pan which has been oiled with vegetable spray. Bake for 30 minutes. Let cool for 10 minutes, before slicing.

***Note**: To make your own curry powder (see page 117).

Eggplant & Lamb

The French name for eggplant is "aubergine". Whatever you choose to call it, the purple vegetable has an affinity for lamb. This is a complete meal and very filling. I like to serve this with Pita bread that has been quartered, lightly buttered and filled with freshly grated Parmesan cheese then warmed. 6 servings.

1 pound ground lamb
2 eggplants
$1/4$ cup olive oil
$1/2$ teaspoon salt
$1/4$ teaspoon pepper
2 garlic cloves, peeled and chopped
2 green onions, trimmed and chopped
1 tablespoon parsley, chopped
$1/4$ teaspoon dried rosemary
$1/4$ teaspoon dried marjoram
2 tablespoons tomato purée
$1/4$ cup flour
$1/2$ cup milk
1 egg

Preheat oven to 350°F. Wash and trim eggplants and cut into $1/4$-inch slices. Heat olive oil in a skillet and brown slices on both sides. Drain on paper towels. Add garlic and onions to pan and sauté until soft. Add lamb and sauté until browned. Add spices and tomato purée. Simmer for 10 minutes, stirring frequently.

Place a layer of eggplant slices into a greased casserole. Pour meat mixture over eggplant, cover meat with another layer of eggplant. Combine flour, milk and egg in top of a double boiler. Whisk over simmering water until thickened, then pour the sauce over eggplant. Bake for 30 minutes.

Lamb in Grape Leaves

No book on lamb is worth its salt unless there is a recipe
calling for the traditional grape leaves. 6 servings of two each.

$^1/_2$ pound ground lamb
3 tablespoons olive oil
$^1/_2$ cup finely chopped white onions
1 cup raw rice
1 teaspoons finely chopped fresh mint **or** $^1/_2$ teaspoon dried
$^1/_4$ teaspoon cinnamon
$^1/_2$ teaspoon salt
12 grape leaves-fresh* or 1 (8-ounce) jar (available
 on the specialty items shelf at your grocery store)
Water as needed
$^1/_2$ cup fresh lemon juice
Lemon wedges

Preheat oven to 350°F. Heat oil in a skillet and sauté onions,
rice and mint until onion is soft and rice a golden brown,
approximately 10 minutes. Add lamb, cinnamon and salt,
mixing well.

Place a heaping tablespoon of the lamb mixture on a grape
leaf and roll, folding in the ends. Pack the stuffed grape
bundles snugly into a casserole, and add a slight amount of
water to prevent them from scorching. Cover and steam in
oven for 1 hour. Before serving, squeeze fresh lemon juice
over and place additional lemon wedges on the side.

*Note: If you use young tender fresh grape leaves, be sure
to wash them thoroughly before using to remove any pests
or pesticides.

Lamb Patties in Custard

A savory dish of contrasting textures! In the spring, steamed asparagus is a perfect vegetable accompaniment. For the fall and winter months, crisp, al dente broccoli flowerettes are nice. Garden-fresh green beans in the summer are perfect. 4 servings.

For Patties:
1 pound ground lamb
1 tablespoon fresh chopped parsley
$^1/_2$ teaspoon salt
$^1/_8$ teaspoon pepper
$^1/_2$ small onion, chopped finely
1 clove garlic, pressed
1 teaspoon paprika
1 tablespoon vegetable oil

For Custard:
4 large eggs
$^1/_2$ cup low-fat yogurt **or** sour cream
$^1/_2$ teaspoon salt
$^1/_8$ teaspoon pepper

Preheat oven to 350°F. Mix the first seven ingredients well and shape into four (1$^1/_2$-inch-thick) patties. Heat the oil in a frying pan and sear patties on both sides until crisp and browned. Pour off excess fat. Transfer patties to a shallow baking dish.

Break eggs into a small bowl and whisk lightly. Add yogurt and spices and whisk, until blended. Pour mixture over patties. Bake for 1 hour, or until the custard is set.

Lemon Lamb Patties

Keep the fat content low by draining fat often. Ground lamb has the same taste as an expensive cut for less than half the price. 4 servings.

1 pound ground lamb
$^1/_2$ cup water
$^1/_4$ cup lemon juice
Grated peel of a fresh lemon
$^1/_2$ teaspoon pepper

Mix ground lamb with all ingredients and shape into four 3-inch patties. Preheat a small skillet and fry the patties over medium heat, turning once, until crisp on the outside and *slightly* pink on the inside.

Baked Lamb Meatballs

Nicely spiced. 4 servings (entrée), 8 servings (appetizers).

1 pound ground lamb
$^1/_2$ cup dry bread crumbs
$^1/_2$ cup milk
1 egg
1 small onion, chopped
1 garlic clove, peeled and crushed
1 tablespoon fresh chopped mint leaves **or** $^1/_2$ teaspoon dried
$^1/_2$ teaspoon oregano
1 teaspoon salt to taste
1 teaspoon pepper

Mix all ingredients and shape into small balls. Place meatballs on an ungreased jelly roll pan or a 13 x 9-inch baking pan. (Line with aluminum foil for easy clean up). Cook, uncovered, in a 350°F oven, until brown for 25 minutes.

Speedy Curried Meatballs

When I'm in a hurry, the microwave oven comes through. These meatballs are good over a bed of plain white rice. Toss a salad, and dinner is ready. 4 servings.

1 pound ground lamb
1 garlic clove, minced
1 medium onion, sliced
1 celery stalk, sliced
2 tablespoons flour
1¹/₂ tablespoons curry powder
¹/₂ teaspoon salt
2 chicken bouillon cubes, crushed
³/₄ cup water
¹/₄ cup any chutney
1 teaspoon prepared mustard

Mix lamb and garlic in a 1¹/₂-quart, or larger, mixing bowl. Form into 1-inch balls and arrange in a microwave-safe dish in one layer. Add onion and celery and cook, uncovered, for 5 minutes on HIGH (100% power). Turn dish once halfway through cooking time. Drain off fat; sprinkle the meatballs with flour, curry powder and crushed bouillon cubes. Mix chutney, mustard and water in a measuring cup and pour over meatballs. Cook, uncovered, for 4 minutes on HIGH, turning and stirring once.

Unforgettable Meatballs

Remember, "Rosemary for Remembrance"? Don't forget to
use rosemary in any ground lamb dish for an unforgettable,
almost Mediterranean flavor. Serve over spinach noodles.
6 servings.

1½ pounds ground lamb
½ cup fresh bread crumbs
2 garlic cloves, peeled and chopped
1 tablespoon dried rosemary **or** 2 tablespoons fresh
1 teaspoon salt
½ teaspoon pepper
¼ cup grated Parmesan cheese
3 tablespoons olive oil
1 cup chicken stock
2 tablespoons cornstarch

Mix together lamb, crumbs, garlic, rosemary, salt, pepper
and cheese, blending well. Form into 1-inch meatballs. Heat
oil in a large skillet and brown meatballs well. Remove
meatballs and set aside. Using a slotted spoon, scrape all bits
from the bottom of the pan. Combine stock and cornstarch
mixture. Add mixture to pan and stir until thickened. Add
meatballs to pan, stir gently. Adjust seasonings, if necessary.
Simmer meatballs in gravy for 30 minutes.

Variation:

Unforgettable Spaghetti Sauce

Omit the bread crumbs, chicken stock and cornstarch. Add
½ cup chopped onion. Sauté the remaining ingredients,
except cheese, in the oil, until browned. Add 1 can (15-
ounce) whole tomatoes with juice. Simmer 30 minutes. Add
cheese and seasonings to taste. Serve over pasta.

Kidney & Liver

For some reason, the kidneys and the liver of spring lamb are hard to find, but they can be ordered from the meat department. When you have lamb cut to your specifications, remember to tell the butcher to keep them for you. The following recipes are easy to prepare. One is a staple of good English fare and the other is just plain delicious.

Tony's English Mixed Grill

An English-style entrée that my English friend, Tony, often prepared as a special brunch or dinner. Traditionally served with potatoes (hash browns, steamed or mashed) and fried tomato slices. Don't forget the English Mint Sauce (page 113) for the chops! 2 servings.

2 rib **or** loin lamb chops, trimmed
4 strips bacon
4 lamb kidneys, cut in $1/2$-inch slices **or** 1 lamb liver, sliced*

Panfry or broil lamb chops. Keep chops warm in oven on serving plates. Fry bacon in large skillet. Drain off bacon fat leaving 1 teaspoon in pan. Sauté kidneys or liver in skillet.

On warmed plates, place kidneys or liver slices next to lamb chop and top with bacon slices.

*Note: Slice liver thinly for quick cooking and the sweetest taste. Liver may be dredged in seasoned flour before frying, if preferred.

Lamb Liver with a Friend

Most women like liver. My theory is that we know it's good for our bodies, adding precious iron to our blood. Invite a friend over and prepare a simple luncheon of sautéed liver and onions, add a fresh green salad, cheesy rolls and a glass of wine to celebrate your womanhood! 2 to 3 servings.

1 pound lamb liver
$^1/_2$ cup flour
$^1/_8$ teaspoon salt **or** garlic salt
$^1/_8$ teaspoon pepper
$^1/_4$ teaspoon paprika
$^1/_4$ teaspoon Beau Monde seasoning
2 tablespoons bacon drippings, butter, margarine **or** oil
$^1/_2$ cup sliced white onion (or more, if desired)

Trim away any membranes from the liver, and rinse under cold water. Cut the liver in $^1/_2$-inch or thinner slices. Combine flour, salt, pepper, paprika and Beau Monde seasoning. Dredge in seasoned flour.

Melt bacon drippings in a heavy skillet and sauté onion slices, until they are transparent. Remove onion with a slotted spoon; place on paper towels to drain. Hold warm. Sauté the seasoned liver slices in the drippings about 2 to 3 minutes per side, or until done. Do not overcook. Serve topped with sautéed onions.

"Cursed with an appetite keen I am,
And I'll subdue it–And I'll subdue it–
With cold roast lamb."

W.S. Gilbert

Lamb Leftovers

Leftovers

When knighthood was in flower, a wandering knight would be received at any castle with a sumptuous meal. However, the common traveller would do well to be offered a plate of cold meat. Since mutton was a common food of the time in England, he would likely get the *cold shoulder*. (Morris Dictionary of Words and Phrases Origins).

Irma S. Rombauer, author of **The Joy of Cooking,** said, "The definition of eternity is two people and one ham." It can be only slightly less time with a leg of lamb. However, there are a number of tasty things to do with cold lamb other than whipping up a curry (although I am going to do just that a little later in this chapter, since everyone likes it).

Apple Lamb

Every kitchen should have these ingredients on hand to make this simple, yet elegant dish. Serve on a bed of white rice.
4 to 6 servings.

2 cups cooked lamb, trimmed of fat and cubed
2 tablespoons olive oil
1 clove garlic, peeled and crushed
1 onion, peeled and chopped
1 medium tomato, chopped
¼ cup apple juice
2 tablespoons curry powder (see page 117)
1 apple, diced
1 tablespoon raisins **or** currants

Heat oil in a large skillet and add the garlic and onion. Cook until soft. Stir in tomato, apple juice and curry powder. Cover and cook for 3 minutes. Add lamb, apple and raisins, and simmer until the lamb is heated through and the apple tender. (Do not overcook).

Fruited Lamb Curry

I promised a curry, and here it is. This is the one my mother made, and the one my husband insists on. It is not a "traditional curry", but certainly has a following! Serve over white rice, and pass the chutney and condiments. 6 servings.

2 cups cooked lamb, trimmed and diced
1 tart apple, unpeeled, cored and diced
$^1/_2$ cup raisins
$^1/_2$ cup chicken broth
1$^1/_2$ tablespoons butter **or** margarine
1 large onion, peeled and diced
1 cup mushrooms, sliced
1 lemon, sliced thin
$^3/_4$ tablespoon curry powder (see page 117)
1$^1/_2$ tablespoons flour
$^1/_2$ to $^3/_4$ cup milk
1 teaspoon salt **or** to taste
1 teaspoon pepper
2 cloves garlic, peeled and chopped

In a small saucepan, simmer apple and raisins in broth until tender. Remove apple pieces and raisins from broth and set aside.

Melt butter in a large skillet and sauté onion, mushrooms and lemon. Add curry powder and flour, stirring well. Slowly add chicken broth. Stir until thickened. Adjust consistency with additional milk, as desired. Add lamb, seasonings and reserved apple and raisins . Heat through.

Lamb in Pepper Cases

Green peppers are wonderful. They hold a variety of things and look attractive doing it. Try them with lamb. 4 servings.

1 cup cooked lamb, trimmed and cubed
4 green peppers, of uniform shapes
Water
$^1/_2$ cup fresh bread crumbs
$^1/_2$ cup chicken bouillon
$^1/_2$ cup chopped tomato
$^1/_2$ teaspoon salt
$^1/_4$ teaspoon pepper
Fresh grated Parmesan cheese

Preheat oven to 350°F. Cut the stems off the tops of peppers and remove seeds. Parboil the peppers for 5 minutes. Remove from water and drain.

Combine lamb with bread crumbs, bouillon, tomato, salt and pepper. Fill pepper cases with lamb mixture. Sprinkle Parmesan cheese on tops. Place in a greased ovenproof pan and bake for 15 minutes.

Lamb Pilaf

This is a staple in most country kitchens. 6 servings.

2 cups cooked lamb, trimmed and cubed
1 medium onion, chopped
1 clove garlic, peeled and chopped
1 tablespoon olive oil
2 cups water
1 cup uncooked white rice
$1/2$ cup chopped green pepper
1 chicken bouillon cube
$1/2$ teaspoon tarragon
$1/2$ teaspoon salt
$1/2$ teaspoon pepper

In a large saucepan, sauté onion and garlic in olive oil, until transparent. Stir in all remaining ingredients. Heat to boiling, reduce heat, cover and cook for 25 to 30 minutes, or until rice is tender and has absorbed the liquid. Fluff with a fork, before serving.

"Who has but one lamb makes it fat."
French proverb

Pasta Lamb

Hearty and robust, this is a favorite with teenagers. It's a very good dish to make ahead of time and freezes well. 6 servings.

2 cups cooked lamb, trimmed of excess fat and cubed
3 tablespoons olive oil
4 cloves of garlic, peeled and chopped
2 pounds Italian-style tomatoes, chopped and drained
$\frac{1}{2}$ teaspoon cayenne pepper
$\frac{1}{2}$ teaspoon salt
$\frac{1}{4}$ teaspoon pepper
$\frac{1}{2}$ cup red wine (optional)
1 pound fresh broccoli, chopped
Pasta
1 cup fresh grated Parmesan cheese

Heat olive oil in a large skillet. Add the garlic and sauté for 1 minute. Add tomatoes, cayenne pepper, salt, pepper, wine and broccoli. Bring to a boil, reduce heat and simmer for 30 minutes. Adjust seasonings, if necessary.

Cook pasta of your choice, drain and add to the warm sauce; toss to combine thoroughly. Sprinkle with Parmesan cheese.

Variation:
1 pound of ground lamb may be substituted for cooked lamb. After sautéing garlic, add ground lamb to the skillet and fry until thoroughly cooked. Proceed as directed.

Popeye's Lamb

This is low in carbohydrates and high in nutrition. It also rates high on the taste scale. 4 servings.

1 pound cooked lamb, trimmed of fat and cubed
3 (10-ounce) packages frozen chopped spinach
  or 2 pounds fresh, cooked and chopped
¼ pound butter **or** margarine, melted
4 tablespoons low-fat mayonnaise
4 tablespoons grated Parmesan cheese
½ teaspoon salt
¼ teaspoon pepper
¼ teaspoon Worcestershire sauce

Preheat oven to 350°F. Cook frozen spinach as directed and drain well. Combine all ingredients in a 2-quart ovenproof casserole. Bake for 30 minutes.

Note: Addtional freshly grated Parmesan cheese may be sprinkled over the top just before serving.

Puget Sound Oysters & Lamb

I grew up on the shores of Puget Sound. My father just loved oysters, and so I learned to eat (and enjoy) them at a very early age. They were cheap and plentiful then, and my mother used them in a variety of ways. Two of my favorites were in the turkey dressing and this innovative recipe that uses leftover lamb. Serve over toast. Garnish with parsley. 6 servings.

1/4 cup butter **or** margarine
1 cup oysters, drained and chopped
1/2 pound fresh mushrooms, washed and sliced
1/2 cup flour
1/2 teaspoon salt
1/4 teaspoon pepper
3/4 teaspoon dried marjoram
2 cups unsalted chicken broth
1 1/2 cups light cream **or** an 8-ounce can of evaporated
  milk (my mother's choice)
6 pieces of toast
1/4 cup fresh parsley, chopped
2 1/2 cups cooked lamb, trimmed of excess fat, cubed

Melt butter in a large skillet. Add oysters. Cook and stir gently for 5 minutes. Remove oysters, using a slotted spoon. Add mushrooms to the pan; cook until tender. Stir in flour, salt, pepper and marjoram. Lower heat and gradually add chicken broth and cream. Cook, stirring until thickened.

Add lamb and heat through. Return oysters to the pan, simmer until heated. Ladle over toast.

Summer Lamb Salad

Cold lamb is appetizing when combined with the crisp veg-etables in this cool and refreshing salad. Try it! I think you will like it. 6 servings.

2 cups cooked lamb, trimmed and cubed
2 cups cooked red potatoes, cooled and diced
1 cup chopped celery
1/2 cup sliced green onions **or** fresh chopped garlic chives
12 crisp lettuce leaves
3 tomatoes quartered
4 tablespoons fresh mint, chopped

Oil & Vinegar Dressing:
1/3 cup olive oil
3 tablespoons any flavored vinegar
1/2 teaspoon salt
1/4 teaspoon white pepper

Whisk oil and vinegar together until smooth. Add salt and pepper and adjust to taste, if necessary.

Combine lamb, potatoes, celery and green onions in a salad bowl. Pour Oil & Vinegar Dressing over and mix gently. Refrigerate for at least one hour before serving to allow the flavors to combine.

Serve on crisp lettuce leaves and garnish with fresh toma-toes. Sprinkle fresh chopped mint over each serving.

"My wife is one of the best wimmin on this continent, altho' she isn't always gentle as a lamb with mint sauce."

Artemus Ward

Accompaniments
& Condiments

Cranberry Chutney

*There are lots of chutneys, but in my book, this is one of the very best. Marsha Peters Johnson, author of **Gourmet Vinegars** and her forthcoming book, **Gourmet Chutneys** (Culinary Arts Ltd., Publishers), shares this exquisite recipe. This spicy, garnet-colored chutney is perfect with roast lamb. Makes 5 to 6 half-pints.*

2 cups whole cranberries
1 cup white, apple cider, white wine **or** cranberry vinegar, divided
2 cups granulated sugar
2 teaspoons ground ginger
1 teaspoon ground cloves
1/4 teaspoon chili powder
5 to 6 drops hot pepper sauce (optional)
1 teaspoon salt
2 garlic cloves, peeled and minced
3 to 4 medium-tart apples (4 to 5 cups), peeled, cored, and diced
1 cup chopped nuts (hazelnuts, almonds, pecans **or** walnuts)

Finely chop cranberries in blender or food processor with part of the vinegar for liquid.

Mix first nine ingredients in a large stainless steel pot with lid. Heat to boiling, stirring constantly, then add apples. Simmer 30 minutes or until thick, stirring occasionally. Add nuts and cool.

Store in refrigerator for up to 4 weeks or freeze up to six months. To can: pack in hot, sterile jars, leaving 1/2-inch headspace. Process jars in a boiling-water bath, for 10 minutes.

Mint Chutney

This recipe is designed to give lamb chops and steaks gourmet flair. Courtesy of the American Sheep Industry Association. Makes 1 cup.

¹/₄ cup finely chopped onion
¹/₃ cup white wine vinegar
¹/₃ cup mint jelly
¹/₂ cup golden raisins
¹/₄ cup finely chopped crystallized ginger **or** ¹/₄ teaspoon
  ground ginger

Combine onion and vinegar in small saucepan. Bring to a boil. Reduce heat; cover and simmer for 3 minutes. Add jelly, raisins and ginger. Boil, uncovered, for 3 minutes. Pour into a bowl. Cover and chill at least 2 hours before serving.

Apple-Mint Chutney

This is a true Northwest chutney, cool and refreshing. Wonderful for a gift, as well as a superb lamb accompaniment. Try it with cream cheese and crackers as an appetizer. Makes 1 cup.

1 cup fresh mint leaves*, washed and torn
1 small, tart apple (such as Granny Smith), left unpeeled and
  coarsely chopped
1 small white onion, peeled and coarsely chopped
$1/2$ cup hazelnuts, chopped
3 tablespoons fresh parsley, minced
1 teaspoon salt
1 tablespoon sugar
$1/4$ teaspoon cayenne
$1/2$ teaspoon curry powder
1 tablespoon lemon juice

In a blender or food processor, chop the mint, apple, onion, hazelnuts, parsley, salt, sugar, cayenne and curry, scraping down the sides of the blender frequently, until chutney is finely chopped and blended together. Add lemon juice and blend again. Adjust seasonings to taste. Chill at least 2 hours, before serving.

*Note: Use either peppermint, spearmint or any other type of mint from your garden. A blend of mints is excellent, too. If you have a special mint, like apple-mint, even better! Select only the young top leaves. The bottom (older ones) and stems add a bitter taste, and do not chop as well.

English Mint Sauce

*Taste this sauce and you'll know why the English won't eat lamb without it. This economical and authentic recipe comes from **Easy Microwave Preserving***. *It takes just minutes to prepare this English classic. Serve to taste over any lamb chop, steak or roast. Makes ²/₃ cup.*

3 tablespoons water
2 tablespoons sugar
¹/₂ cup finely chopped mint leaves **or** ¹/₄ cup dried
¹/₃ cup vinegar (white wine **or** champagne vinegar best)

In a 2-cup glass measure, combine water and sugar. Microwave on HIGH (100% power) for 45 seconds. Stir to make sure the sugar is dissolved. Allow to cool. Add remaining ingredients. Stir well and allow to 'rest' ¹/₂ hour. Serve.

Notes: For longer storage, place sauce in a tightly-capped glass bottle and store at room temperature.

May be prepared conventionally in saucepan over medium heat.

*Reprinted with permission from EASY MICROWAVE PRESERVING, ©1992 by Cynthia Fischborn & Cheryl Long, published by The Globe Pequot Press, Old Saybrook, CT 06475.

Mint Riata

The sauce-like riata is a cool and refreshing complement to spicy lamb dishes like curry. Makes 2 cups.

2 cloves garlic, peeled and pressed
1 cup low-fat plain yogurt
2 tablespoons fresh mint, washed and chopped fine
  or 1 tablespoon dried
1/4 cup onion, peeled and finely chopped
1 small cucumber, peeled and finely chopped
  (English or "burpless" variety preferred)

Press garlic directly into yogurt. Stir in mint, onion and cucumber. Refrigerate at least 1 hour before serving.

Variations:

Mint Salad

Add 1/2 cup raw, chopped vegetables such as broccoli, carrots, peppers, raisins, green beans or tomatoes to the yogurt mixture for a cool and colorful salad. 2 to 4 servings.

Mint Soup

Thin riata with 1 1/2 cups buttermilk or additional yogurt, and this becomes a wonderful first course soup. Garnish with a fresh mint leaf. 4 servings.

Mint Stuffing

As long as we are on the subject of mint (did I mention that I have quite a bit in my herb garden?), here is another good thing to do with mint. It is good served with lamb, chicken or fish! Makes 4 cups.

3 tablespoons butter **or** margarine
¼ cup chopped onion
¼ cup chopped celery
1 teaspoon salt
½ teaspoon pepper
½ cup fresh mint leaves, washed and chopped
  or ¼ cup dried mint
3 tablespoons melted butter **or** margarine
3 cups dry bread crumbs

Preheat oven to 350°F. Melt the first 3 tablespoons of butter in a saucepan. Sauté onion and celery. Add seasonings and mint. Cook until liquid is evaporated.

Mix in the last 3 tablespoons of melted butter and bread crumbs. Mix together thoroughly. Bake in a greased casserole for 20 minutes.

Note: Uncooked stuffing may be used in fish filets, pounded skinless chicken breasts or a rolled boneless lamb.

Emerald Mint Jelly

Because of its cool and moist climate, Oregon is the largest grower of mint in the United States. In fact, 60% of the mint used for domestic consumption is grown in the Willamette Valley, Central Oregon and on the Oregon-Idaho border. Each growing area has its own distinctive flavor. Mint is a hardy perennial herb and some of the fields are over twenty years old! Peppermint is the favorite mint to use in this classic mint jelly that has the Oregon Mint Commission's seal of approval. Makes 4 half-pint jars.

3 pounds tart light-colored apples **or** crabapples,
  to make 4 cups juice
3 cups sugar
1 cup washed and chopped fresh mint **or** 1/4 cup dried
2 drops green vegetable food coloring (optional)

Wash and cut apples into 2-inch pieces. Place apples in a large heavy saucepan; add sufficient water to cover. Cover and cook about 15 minutes, or until juice flows, crushing apples with a heavy spoon occasionally. Strain cooked apples and juice through several layers of cheesecloth over a large bowl. This yields about 4 cups of juice.

Return juice to a heavy saucepan. Bring it to a boil and continue boiling for 5 minutes, stirring frequently. Add sugar, mint and food coloring. Boil for an additional 15 minutes, or until the mixture jells. (Test by using the back of a wooden spoon-if it coats the spoon and doesn't run easily, it's jelly). Remove from heat. Skim off foam and pour jelly into hot sterilized jars. Seal immediately.

Curry As You Like It

What exactly is curry? The powder is a personalized combination of herbs and spices. Cayenne and coriander seem to determine the amount of heat or "bite" in the finished product. The word 'curry' comes from the Hindu word, 'turcarri', meaning sauce. The English word applies to any kind of Indian stew in which meats or vegetables are simmered with spices. Pickles, chopped nuts, shredded coconut, chutneys and crackers are traditional side dishes to a curry.

I like this curry powder blend that was developed by Helene Sawyer, author of **Gourmet Mustards** *(Culinary Arts Ltd., Publishers). The degree of 'hotness' will vary with the amount of cayenne pepper. Makes ¹/₂ cup.*

2 tablespoons coriander seeds
1 tablespoon cumin seeds
1 tablespoon yellow mustard seeds
¹/₂ tablespoon fenugreek seeds

In a microwave-safe shallow dish, microwave all the above seeds on HIGH (100% power) for 7 minutes, or until spices exude a smoky aroma and have turned several shades darker. Stir two to three times during cooking time. Remove from microwave. When completely cool, grind into a fine powder.

Add:
1 tablespoon dry mustard
1 tablespoon tumeric
1 tablespoon cayenne pepper
1 tablespoon fresh ground black pepper
¹/₂ tablespoon white pepper

Transfer to an airtight jar and store in a dark cool place. Use in your favorite vegetable dish or meat curry recipe.

Daffodil Rice

This pretty dish got its name from a little friend who came to dinner, and upon viewing it for the first time, proclaimed it as "Daffodil Rice!" It gets the distinctive color from saffron, a spice that is costly, but since I use so little and not very often, has paid me back many times. Make this ahead of time and re-heat it while your roast is 'resting'. 4 servings.

2 tablespoons butter **or** margarine
$^{1}/_{2}$ cup onion, chopped
1 cup raw, white long-grained rice
2 cups water
2 chicken bouillon cubes **or** equivalent paste
$^{1}/_{4}$ teaspoon saffron threads

Melt butter in a small skillet and sauté onion until transparent. Add rice and stir for 2 to 3 minutes, or until rice is lightly browned. Pour in water, bring to a boil. Stir in bouillon cubes. Add saffron threads, crumbled, mixing thoroughly.

Turn rice mixture into a 1-quart casserole, cover tightly and bake for 30 minutes, or until liquid is absorbed.

Variations:
Add $^{1}/_{2}$ cup golden raisins **or** 2 tablespoons pine nuts.

Eggplant Delight

I happen to like eggplant. I know lots of people who don't, but I can fool them with this casserole. Eggplant is rather bland, but will take on subtle flavors, if given the chance. This is very good with any lamb dish. 6 servings.

1 large eggplant, peeled and cut into $1/2$-inch cubes
1 medium onion, chopped fine
1 cup cracker crumbs
$1 1/4$ cups grated extra-sharp cheddar cheese
1 teaspoon fresh basil, torn into pieces **or** $1/2$ teaspoon dried
$1/2$ teaspoon salt
$1/8$ teaspoon pepper
$1/2$ cup milk

Preheat oven to 350°F. In a large bowl, mix together eggplant, chopped onion, cracker crumbs, grated cheese, basil, salt and pepper. Turn into a greased casserole and pour milk over all. Cover and bake for 40 minutes.

Roasted Potatoes
with Garlic & Rosemary

When you are planning that special leg of lamb dinner, consider this as a side dish. It is simple, aromatic and pleases just about everybody. 6 servings.

1 tablespoon olive oil
2 pounds red potatoes, quartered
4 cloves of garlic, peeled and sliced
2 teaspoons fresh rosemary, crumbled **or** 1 teaspoon dried

In a small bowl, place garlic in olive oil. Set aside. Put potatoes in a saucepan and cover with water; bring to a boil and cook until potatoes are tender, about 15 minutes. Drain.

Place cooked potatoes in a shallow dish or pie pan. Pour the garlic-flavored oil over them, discard garlic slices. Sprinkle rosemary over. Broil until browned, about 7 minutes.

Note: Potatoes may be arranged around lamb roast during the final 30 minutes of roasting time. Turn once or twice.

Tuscany White Bean Casserole

This recipe came to me by way of our son, who lived in Tuscany for 6 months. I recommend that you make this a day ahead of time. The flavors mix together, making it simple to reheat, while the lamb roast is 'resting'. 12 servings.

1 pound dried Great Northern beans
Boiling water
$^2/_3$ cup water
1 cup chopped onion
$^1/_4$ cup chopped celery and leaves
3 tablespoons olive oil
1 teaspoon salt
4 garlic cloves, peeled and crushed
$^1/_4$ cup fresh sage leaves **or** $^1/_3$ cup dried
1 ($13^3/_4$-ounce) can chicken broth
4 tablespoons fresh lemon juice
$^1/_2$ teaspoon pepper

Place beans in a large casserole and cover with boiling water 2-inch above the beans.

Let stand for 1 hour. Drain beans. Return beans to casserole and combine with $^2/_3$ cup water, onion, celery, oil, salt, garlic, sage and broth. Stir well. Cover and bake at 375°F for 2 hours or until beans are very tender. Stir in lemon juice and pepper. Adjust seasonings, if necessary.

Variation:

Tuscany Bean Soup

This recipe makes a lot of beans. The next day, add additional chicken broth and lemon juice to thin beans to soup consistency. This freezes well. The full recipe will provide 12 to 16 servings, but smaller quantities can be made with leftover beans.

Baby Artichokes with Hazelnuts

The Oregon Hazelnut Marketing Board shares a recipe that is, I think, a perfect side dish to lamb. 6 servings.

12 baby artichokes
¼ cup olive oil
1½ cups chopped red onion
1¼ cups chopped hazelnuts
1 cup dry white wine
¼ cup fresh crumbled oregano **or** 2 tablespoons dried
¼ cup fresh chopped parsley **or** 2 tablespoons dried
1 teaspoon salt
½ teaspoon pepper

Rinse artichokes and remove tough outer leaves. Cut off stems and top quarter of each artichoke. Cut them in half. Heat olive oil in a sauté pan and sauté artichokes for 8 minutes. Add onion and chopped hazelnuts. Continue cooking until onion is tender. Add wine, oregano, parsley and mix thoroughly. Adjust seasonings, if necessary.

Nearly Irish Bread

*I have no idea where I got this recipe - it's been handwritten in
the back of one of my cookbooks for years and years. I make it
several times during the year, not just for St. Patrick's Day. It's
good with marmalade for Sunday breakfast, and it goes well
with the Irish Stews (see pages 74-78). Serve in wedge-shaped
pieces with unsalted butter. Makes 1 loaf.*

1 baking powder biscuit dough recipe
  (Increase the butter **or** margarine by 2 tablespoons
  and the sugar by 1 tablespoon)
$^1/_2$ cup raisins
$^1/_2$ cup currants
1 tablespoon caraway seeds

Preheat oven to 350°F. Mix all ingredients together and turn
out onto a floured board. Knead 10 times. Shape dough into
a flat ball.

Bake in an oiled round cake pan or an iron skillet (which is
even more authentic) for 30 minutes. Increase oven temperature to 400°F for last 5 minutes.

Index

Index

Index

* Denotes microwave recipe.

Lamb Country Cooking, and other cookbooks published by Culinary Arts Ltd., may be found in book, cooking, gift, herb and specialty stores.

If you have difficulty finding a title in your area, please contact the publisher for information.

Culinary Arts Ltd.
Publishers of Unique Specialty Books
P.O. Box 2157
Lake Oswego, OR 97035

Phone: 503-639-4549
Fax: 503-620-4933